The Fangirl's Guide to the Galaxy

# THE FANGIRL'S GUIDE TO THE GALAXY

## a handbook for GEEK GIRLS

### by SAM MAGGS

QUIRK BOOKS
PHILADELPHIA

Copyright © 2015 by Sam Maggs

Library of Congress Cataloging in Publication Number:
2014909460

ISBN: 978-1-59474-789-2

Printed in China
Typeset in Avenir, Blaue Brush, and RidemyBike Serif

Designed by Andie Reid
Illustrations by Kelly Bastow
Production management by John J. McGurk

Quirk Books
215 Church Street
Philadelphia, PA 19106
quirkbooks.com

10 9 8 7 6 5 4 3 2 1

## To my mom
my ultimate convention buddy,
biggest supporter,
and the best fangirl I know

## And to my dad
who sat me down as a toddler
to play *Doom* and *Myst* together,
which made me love games forever

# Contents

# One of Us!
# One of Us!

# I'm a fangirl.

More often than not, people hit me with that word in a derogatory way. They use it to make me feel devalued, unintelligent, and immature. And you know what? They couldn't be more wrong.

*Being a fangirl is the best thing that's ever happened to me.* My geekiness has made me friends all over the world, women who continue to be the most intelligent, well-spoken, and wonderful people I know. Fandom has given me a voice to advocate for the things I'm passionate about. And being a geek girl is constantly exciting—no one else gets more invested in the things they love. New video game? Freak out for months in advance over the cover art! Waiting for a new season of *Sherlock*? Create an endless number of GIFs to ease your pain! Angry about the way they posed Black Widow on that new poster? She-Hulk smash the patriarchy! What's more, regardless of their particular fandom, geek girls are devoted to supporting women in media, constantly pushing an agenda of acceptance, diversity, and fair representation. Oh, and we manage to do all this while containing our squees. Mostly.

We know what we're into, we love hard, and we're okay with it. But we don't have it easy.

Far too often, fangirls are made to feel marginalized and unwelcome in the nerd community. Women are ostracized from online gaming, called out as fake, accused of being desperate for attention, harassed while cosplaying, and, worst of all, forced into silence. Some dude nerds don't like that we're invading their space and have become obsessed with gatekeeping, deciding who "counts" as a real fan and who doesn't. *You're not a true fan if you only like the Marvel movies; you can't be in the anime community unless you speak fluent Japanese; you're not allowed to dress up as Ms. Marvel unless you've read every Ms. Marvel comic, ever.* I once had a comic-book-store employee refuse to help me unless I could name everyone who had ever been a member of the Avengers. Do you know how many superheroes that is? It's *a lot*. Do you think he ever asked that of a guy in the shop? I'm gonna go with "nah, son," because you *know* that never happened.

But you know what's really crazy about all that? More and more, nerdy audiences are made up of literal Bat-tons of fangirls. (Because, spoiler alert: basically half of all fans of anything are ladies.) According to a 2014 survey by the Entertainment Software Association, female gamers age 18 and up make up 36% of the gaming population, compared to just 17% for boys age 17 and under, and in recent years over half the social media discussions at San Diego Comic-Con were generated from accounts run by geek girls. The Syfy channel gets huge ratings with women ages 18–34, thanks in part to lady-driven and LGBT-friendly shows like *Lost Girl*, *Continuum*, *Bitten*, and *Haven*. Women are becoming the driving force behind geek culture, and we shouldn't be relegated to the sidelines.

Knowing that we could basically make our own army, bust down the elitist gatekeepers, and establish our own glorious kingdom (queendom?) of lady-nerds honestly makes me wonder why the hell we haven't done that yet. We're getting better at it—we're taking up more and more space online, we're fighting back against the trolls, and we're refusing to be silent. Merriam-Webster even added "fangirl" to the dictionary. We're fully legit now.

But despite all the articles online about being an awesome nerd-girl, the great feminist Tumblr posts about *Sailor Moon*, and bands like the Doubleclicks receiving worldwide attention, something was still missing: an actual printed book that says, "Being a geek girl is the best thing ever and here are all the ways you can do more nerdy things that are awesome and don't ever apologize for it because you are the best person out there and I'm so proud of you and you're beautiful."

Until now. So here, ladies, is *The Fangirl's Guide to the Galaxy*. I hope in this book you can find some new ideas for your next *Star Wars* premiere party, figure out how to make your IRL bestie the newest member of SuperWhoLock, finally brave your first-ever convention in full cosplay, learn how to start an awesome blog devoted to your craziest ship, and develop the wittiest retort to anyone who ever dares accuse you of being a Fake Geek Girl.

And then you can get back to your *Lord of the Rings* marathon (extended edition, obviously). I promise.

# PAUSE GAME

**Attention, humans!** Although this book is called The *Fangirl's Guide to the Galaxy*, you don't have to be someone who identifies as female to enjoy it! If you consider *yourself* a fan[girl], then this book is for you. (And even if you don't yet, take a looksee through these pages anyways.... You might find yourself becoming a convert.) *One of us! One of us!*

# chapter one

# It's Good to Be a Geek

Greetings, nerdlings! From walking the walk to talking the talk to buying the adorable tie-in T-shirts, we fangirls like to wear our 8-bit hearts on our (sometimes literal) sleeves. If you're shy, never fear: here you will find tips on discovering your geek persona, learning the lingo, and busting out to become the amazing nerd-and-proud lady you've always wanted to be.

# A Field Guide to the Geek Girl

Every fangirl is different. Her very identity as a fangirl is predicated on the fandom that gives her all the feels. But even within fandoms, it would be crazy to assume that I could describe each and every fangirl with accuracy. One fangirl's OTP is another's NOTP; one fangirl likes the reboot and another loves the original. We are all v. v. special and unique, and I love that, so much.

But some fandoms are so popular, they wear their shared squees with pride, and it's almost guaranteed that you're a member of at least *one* of them. Here are the huge-tastic-est fandoms on the Internet, along with their defining characteristics and advice on how to become one (because we all know it can be daunting to embark upon a new quest).

 ## Potterheads or Potterites

**FANDOM:** Harry Potter

**DEFINING CHARACTERISTICS:**

- A deep understanding of the true meaning of friendship

- A voracious and focused ability to read long books

- A love for the Queen, J. K. Rowling

**KEY ACCESSORIES:** Hogwarts crest T-shirt; house scarf of choice; Deathly Hallows tattoo; wand pen; hardcover editions of all seven books; stuffed owl; Potter Puppet Pal; secret piggy bank saving up for a "Wizarding World of Harry Potter" trip; radish earrings; time turner necklace; broom

**HOW TO BECOME ONE:** Read the book that started it all—*Harry Potter and the Philosopher's Stone*—and continue for the next six installments. I know there are movies, but just—just go and read the books.

**UNENDING DEBATES:** Which movie is the best adaptation of the books? Should Hermione have ended up with Ron or Harry? Is Snape a wonderful romantic or a creepy Nice Guy stalker?

 **SuperWhoLockians**

**FANDOM:** *Supernatural* (for Saltgunners), *Doctor Who* (for Whovians), and BBC's *Sherlock* (for Sherlockians)

**DEFINING CHARACTERISTICS:**

➤ An extreme desire for m/m ships to be canon

➤ A love/hate relationship with showrunners

➤ Extreme crushes on every cast member

**KEY ACCESSORIES:** Red hair bow; sonic screwdriver; TARDIS phone case; blue scarf; violin; damask-wallpaper-patterned skirt; keys to an Impala; devil's trap shirt, Dean's skull bracelet

**HOW TO BECOME ONE:** *Sherlock* and *Supernatural* are the easiest—just start with episode one. With *Doctor Who*, you can start with the 2005 reboot pilot "Rose", or you can skip directly to 2011 and go with Matt Smith's first episode "The Eleventh Hour", or you can go back in time (ha!) to the original series, which first aired in 1963.

**UNENDING DEBATES:** *Supernatural*: Are Dean and Castiel totally into each other or nah? *Doctor Who*: Are Steven Moffat's recent seasons the worst or nah? *Sherlock*: Are Sherlock and John totally into each other or nah?

# Ringers, Tolkienites, or Tolkiendils

**FANDOM:** *Lord of the Rings*, *The Hobbit*, all of Tolkien's creations

**DEFINING CHARACTERISTICS:**

- Frequent meal breaks (can you say *second breakfast*?)
- Acceptance and/or love of hairy feet
- Occasionally hissing *"the precious"*

**KEY ACCESSORIES:** Elvish "not all who wander are lost" tattoo; Evenstar necklace; multiple leather belts; big backpack full of snacks; copies of every book (including the legendarium)

**HOW TO BECOME ONE:** If you're daunted by the length of the LOTR books, pick up *The Hobbit* for a quick introduction to Middle-earth and a good read. If you're an aspiring completionist, try *The Silmarillion* (or dive even further with *The Tolkien Reader*). If you want to check out the movies, start with *The Fellowship of the Ring*.

**UNENDING DEBATES:** Why are there so few ladies in LOTR? Did *The Hobbit* really need to be three separate movies? Is Tauriel awesome, even though she isn't canon in the books? (Spoiler: yes.) Why couldn't Gandalf just send eagles with the rings to Mt. Doom?

# Otaku

**FANDOM:** Anime and manga. (Please note that *otaku*, although a typically acceptable term in the West, is still considered potentially derogatory in Japan. I mean it here only in the very best way possible, like "geek" or "nerd.")

- The ability to sit through 200-plus episodes of one show
- A working knowledge of common Japanese terms
- An expert ability to glomp (with consent)

**KEY ACCESSORIES:** Dragonball earrings; Sailor Moon fuku tank; Ein and Appa plushies; Nami's arm tattoo; Death Note notebook; bag with SNK patch, Flamel symbol, and gym badges

**HOW TO BECOME ONE:** The worlds of anime and manga are vast, and they can certainly be daunting. For an introduction to manga, *Sailor Moon* is a classic (and a gateway drug to the magical girl genre at large); pick up the new Kodansha translations first. For anime, dive into a show that has a finite number of episodes—*Cowboy Bebop*, overwhelmingly thought of as one of the all-time bests, comes in at just twenty-six half-hour episodes (or "sessions") and a movie.

**UNENDING DEBATES:** Subs or dubs? The old version of the anime or the remake? The anime or the manga? Pokémon or Yu-Gi-Oh!?

 ## Trekkies or Trekkers

**FANDOM:** *Star Trek* in all its various, glorious iterations.

**DEFINING CHARACTERISTICS:**

- An extreme aversion to red tops
- Expert Vulcan salute
- Yelling "KHAAAAAAAN!" whenever frustrated

**KEY ACCESSORIES:** Uhura's comms officer dress; closed communicator phone case; Starfleet Combadge earrings; bat'leth necklace; tiny noise-making replica tribble

**HOW TO BECOME ONE:** Diehard Trekkies may disagree, but I'd start with the 2009 J. J. Abrams film *Star Trek*: it stars a veritable lunch buffet of hotties and, since it's a reboot, you don't need any prior Trek knowledge to enjoy it. If you want to get into one of the shows, you've got two good points of entry: *Star Trek: The Next Generation*, a classic, starring Patrick Stewart and a lovable band of crewmates, or *Star Trek: Voyager*, the only *Trek* with a female starship captain, and my personal fave *Trek* of all time.

**UNENDING DEBATES:** TOS or TNG? For that matter, Kirk or Picard? Why did *Star Trek: Enterprise* have to happen? Is there any way to order tea other than "Earl Grey, hot"? *Star Trek* or *Star Wars* (and does it matter now that J.J. Abrams does both?)

# Star Warriors

**FANDOM:** *Star Wars*—yes, even the prequels

**DEFINING CHARACTERISTICS:**

➤ A megacrush on Han Solo

➤ A simultaneous respect and disdain for George Lucas

➤ A rabid and intense hatred of Jar Jar Binks

**KEY ACCESSORIES:** Rebel Alliance tank top; headphones that look like Princess Leia buns; lightsaber finger tattoo; Yoda backpack

**HOW TO BECOME ONE:** Start with *Episode IV: A New Hope* and make your way through the original trilogy. (Even though you're technically starting in the middle of the franchise, so did the rest of the world—it's the film that came first—so it doesn't matter.) Once you've fallen in love with the original trilogy (Episodes IV, V, and VI), then you can watch the more recent prequel films (Episodes I, II, and III) and comment on their epic inferiority. And don't neglect the awesomeness that is the TV show *Star Wars: The Clone Wars*.

**UNENDING DEBATES:** Can we all just agree that Han shot first? Did George Lucas *really* always know that Luke and Leia were going to be siblings? Which of the prequels is the *worst* of the prequels? (*Attack of the Clones*, FYI.)

 ## The Unsullied and Bookwalkers

**FANDOM:** *Game of Thrones* (the show) and *A Song of Ice and Fire* (the books). The Unsullied are show fans who haven't read the books, while the Bookwalkers know what's coming way in advance.

**DEFINING CHARACTERISTICS:**

> A desperate desire for baby dragons of your very own

> The knowledge that all men must die

> An understandable aversion to weddings

**KEY ACCESSORIES:** House necklace; intricately braided hair; dragon ear cuffs; huskies; dragon egg leggings; very uncomfortable chair; torn-up wedding invites

**HOW TO BECOME ONE:** If you want half the time commitment (and half the detail), watch the show; otherwise, start with *A Song of Ice and Fire*, book one, *A Game of Thrones*, and prepare to spend the rest of your year (or life) finishing the series.

UNENDING DEBATES: Who will end up sitting on the Iron Throne? Who is Jon Snow's father? Will *anyone* survive the entire series? Are the changes to female characters on the show okay, or are they unfair?

 ## True Believers or Marvelites

FANDOM: Marvel comics and cinematic universe

DEFINING CHARACTERISTICS:

- A passionate love for any of the Avengers
- A healthy respect for Scarlett Johansson
- A reluctance to speak ill of the Spider-Man reboot films

KEY ACCESSORIES: S.H.I.E.L.D. shirt; Black Widow belt; heavily smudged eyeliner; a ring shaped like Cap's shield; Captain Marvel star earrings; Loki-green nail polish

HOW TO BECOME ONE: You can't go wrong starting with the first *Iron Man* movie and heading straight through all the Marvel Cinematic Universe films. If you're just getting into the comics, start with *Runaways*, a series about teenagers who discover their parents are supervillains. Tons of your faves (like Wolverine and Captain America) make guest appearances, it's created by comics genius Brian K. Vaughn, and it's got a few issues written by Joss Whedon himself.

UNENDING DEBATES: Exactly how much better are we than DC? Which Avenger is the ultimate best? How awesome is it that Thor is now a woman? (So awesome.) How can I make everything okay for the Winter Soldier?

# Batgirls

FANDOM: DC comics and films

DEFINING CHARACTERISTICS:

- ᔕ Over-Bat-use of Bat-puns

- ᔕ Nightmares of the Joker showing up at your door à la *The Killing Joke*

- ᔕ The unwavering opinion that Aquaman is really bad-ass

KEY ACCESSORIES: Red shirt, yellow belt, and blue skirt with stars; Bat symbol necklace; Harley Quinn–print purse; cat ear hairband; comic-print heels

HOW TO BECOME ONE: If you're a movie gal, jump in with the Christopher Nolan Batman trilogy (Clooney, I love you, but the nipple-suits were way weird). If you're into comics, start with any of the trade paperbacks from the New 52 (the reboot that reset all of the DC continuity): pick up the first volume of New 52 *Batwoman* (by J. H. Williams III and W. Haden Blackman) and the first volume of New 52 *Batgirl* (by Gail Simone), but also go for New 52 *Aquaman*, *Animal Man*, and *Swamp Thing*, if you're feeling adventurous.

UNENDING DEBATES: Exactly how much better are we than Marvel? Batman or Superman? Batman *versus* Superman? Is Batfleck going to be awesome, or will it be a ginormous mistake? Why does everyone have to think Aquaman is so terrible?

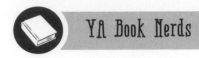

# YA Book Nerds

**FANDOM:** Young adult literature

**DEFINING CHARACTERISTICS:**

> A love for star-crossed couples, especially in trilogy form

> Chronic post-book feeling hangovers

> Ability to walk and read a book at the same time

**KEY ACCESSORIES:** "Okay? Okay." shirt; bird tattoo; mockingjay pin; trident hairpiece; Angelic rune necklace; infinity symbol ring; dragon-eye ring

**HOW TO BECOME ONE:** Read! Beyond the best sellers, Ally Condie's *Matched*, Kiera Cass's *The Selection*, and Lauren Oliver's *Delirium* trilogies are great for dystopia. Want Victorian zombies? Susan Dennard's *Something Strange and Deadly*. Swoony spaceship romance? Beth Revis's *Across the Universe*. A beautifully written exploration of the afterlife? Victoria Schwab's *The Archived*.

**UNENDING DEBATES:** Team Gale or Team Peeta? Why exactly did the world need factions/districts, again? How did *An Imperial Affliction* actually end?

# Whedonites

**FANDOM:** The Whedonverse: anything made by our master, Joss Whedon (*Buffy the Vampire Slayer*, *Angel*, *Firefly*, *Dollhouse*, *Dr. Horrible's Sing-Along Blog...*)

## DEFINING CHARACTERISTICS:

> ➤ A very particular cadence to their speechifying

> ➤ A hatred of the FOX network

> ➤ An wild devotion in their eyes when someone mentions Joss

**KEY ACCESSORIES:** Brown coat, cross necklace, tight leather pants, Captain Hammer's T-shirt, Jayne's knit hat, box of Fruity Oaty bars, the Watcher tome, tears (over the Firefly cancellation)

**HOW TO BECOME ONE:** It's a bit dated, but you can't go wrong starting at the start with Buffy season one. If that's too many seasons for you, grab the nearest Firefly box set and prepare to become instantly obsessed. If you've already seen every episode six times (guilty!), check out the *Buffy the Vampire Slayer Season Eight* comics published by Dark Horse and produced by Joss himself.

**UNENDING DEBATES:** Spike or Angel? *Buffy* or *Angel*? *Why why why why did FOX cancel Firefly*?!

 **Girls Who Game**

**FANDOM:** Gaming. Obv.

**DEFINING CHARACTERISTICS:**

> ➤ Eyes that don't tire after a full-day gaming binge

> ➤ A colorful repertoire of anti-troll responses

> ➤ Carpal tunnel syndrome

**KEY ACCESSORIES:** Gaming headset and tricked-out gaming PC; handheld gaming device of choice; Companion Cube earrings; N7 hoodie; Triforce tattoo; space invader hair clip; Game Boy dress; big, stuffed 1-Up mushroom; a cat named Dovahkiin

**HOW TO BECOME ONE:** Pick up a PS3 or Xbox 360 for cheap and starting playing your way through the massive back catalogue of games available for either system. Just because games aren't brand-new doesn't mean they're not still awesome! If you like fantasy or games with good storylines and characterization, *Dragon Age: Origins* is a great choice; you can try *Little Big Planet* if you want a cute platformer or *Portal* if you're into a good puzzle game.

**UNENDING DEBATES:** Super Nintendo or Sega Genesis? PC or console? Does *The Sims* count as a game? (Answer: absolutely.)

 # Disnerds

**FANDOM:** Disney

**DEFINING CHARACTERISTICS:**

- Hard-core nostalgia for childhood movie-watching

- Encyclopedic knowledge of song lyrics

- Big dreams, big eyes, big hair

**KEY ACCESSORIES:** Huge DVD collection, endless array of princess-themed accessories, flowing locks; stuffed sidekick plushies (Flounder, Olaf, Mushu, Pascal, Meeko, etc.)

**HOW TO BECOME ONE:** You probably grew up watching all the classic Disney films, but you can't go wrong with a marathon rewatch—I guarantee you'll remember the songs. For more modern girl-power Disney flicks, start with *Frozen*, because Elsa.

**UNENDING DEBATES:** Traditional animation or digital? First wave, "golden age," or modern classics? Is *Beauty and the Beast* romantic, or is there some Stockholm syndrome? Is Elsa queer, or does she marry Jack Frost? Could Mulan *be* any more bad-ass?

This list is far from comprehensive! Shout-outs to all my Gleeks, Fannibals, Nerdfighters, Marshmallows, Gaters, Scapers, Wolfers, Oncers, Atimers, Irrelevants, Interns, Castillions, Madokies, Walker Stalkers, Assassins, Smashers, Merlinians, Squints, Toasters, Dreadfuls, Queen's Readers, Homestucks, Jaegers, Moonies, Initiates, Gearheads, Truebies, Titans, Human Beings, X-Philes, Cortexifans, Psych-Os, Hetalians, Sleepyheads, Rum Runners, Jancites, Shadowhunters, Bleachers, Wingnuts, Suitors, Lostralians, Arrowheads, Scoobies, Roomfriends, Pinenuts, Digifans, Evageeks, Lawsbians, the Clone Club, the Carol Corps, and all the other lovely fandoms out there.

# Real Talk: How Do I Fangirl-Speak?

Have you ever lost the ability to can? Do you often find yourself overwhelmed with feels? Are your favorite phrases of endearment laden with violently epic curses? If so, congratulations—you already understand fangirl-speak, the language of choice for geeky gals all around the world. But if you are intimidated or confused by the way fandom communicates, don't worry, you're not alone. It's basically like learning an entirely new subset of the English language, but it's hilarious and completely relevant to all the things you love.

Now, the media, trolls, and Smaug (probably, if Smaug was actually the evil Smaug from the books and not the uncomfortably attractive CumberSmaug from the movies) have written whole diatribes about how fangirl slang sounds stupid, illiterate, frivolous, and shallow. But look at it this way: geek girls—a whole international community of women—have come together online to develop our own means of communication. And that's awesome.

DISCLAIMER: The intarwebs moves fast (which is probably why I can never get any work done). The following list is made up of the most prevalent, long-lasting, and currently relevant terms, so if you go online and see something that isn't here, I'm sorry. But that's part of what makes fangirl-speak so rad.

## Canon and Headcanon

"Canon" describes characters, pairings, events, etc., that are accepted as part of a fictional universe's "official" mythology, as presented either through dramatization in an episode/movie/novel or in officially sanctioned ephemera. The term was first used in reference to Arthur Conan Doyle's Sherlock Holmes series to distinguish Doyle's writings from the myriad other authors who used Holmes's character in their own stories (so, Sherlockians, we can thank you for this one). If you have an idea that branches off from official canon, but that you have decided to accept as personally true, you call that your "headcanon" or, sometimes, "fanon."

EXAMPLE: Sherlock plays violin, wears scarves, and lives at 221B Baker Street? Canon. John Watson likes to dance to Nicki Minaj when he isn't helping solve cases? Headcanon. (For now.)

# Feels ♥♥

Fangirls tend to have a lot of feelings…so many, in fact, that we shorten the word to "feels." When something in fiction affects you on a deep, emotional level, it's *hitting you right in the feels* or, alternately, *giving you all the feels*. (Surprisingly, the term has been around since at least 1782, when Georgiana, Duchess of Devonshire, wrote in a letter to her mother that her "feels" made her cry and gave her insomnia, similar to how a modern fangirl might feel after finishing the Mass Effect trilogy.) Feels can also be spelled phonetically as "pheals" or "pheels," according to your preference. Just do what *feels* right.

EXAMPLE: The end of *Harry Potter and the Deathly Hallows* gave me such feels. All the feels. Every last feel.

# Glomp

A very enthusiastic hug, also known as the combination tackle-hug. The tackle-hug is most frequently seen in anime and manga; the word "glomp" (the word "glom," as in "to grab," with an added "p" for effect) originated in early manga translations from Viz Media, who attached it as a sound effect to artistically rendered tackle-hugs. Glomps are particularly appropriate when meeting an

Internet friend IRL or when you just really, really like someone (so long as you have permission, in either case).

EXAMPLE: "I haven't seen you in ages, friend!" *glomp*

# GPOY

An acronym for "gratuitous picture of yourself," this term can tag either a real selfie (looking good, fangirl!) or something ridiculous that you feel is an accurate representation of yourself or your current mood (e.g., an overfed cat sleeping sprawled out on her back; a screenshot of Kaiju rampaging through the streets of Hong Kong). Can also be used interchangeably with the phrase "me IRL."

EXAMPLE: [A GIF of Usagi Tsukino nomming dumplings, or a particularly cute selfie] GPOY.

# I'm Done

This wonderful multipurpose phrase can be used to express everything from extreme joy to intense anger. When you're "done," you just can't contribute any more to a particular conversation for any number of reasons. It can be good or bad; context is key.

Variations include "I can't," "I have lost the ability to can" or "I am unable to can," "help," "dead," "I'm dying," "Jesus take the wheel," "weeping," "plz," and so on. "What is air" is a particularly beautiful way of expressing that you're laughing so hard, you're no longer able to breathe.

EXAMPLE: "I just saw a super-hot GIF of Benedict Cumberbatch dancing/a hilarious Tumblr text post/a troll trying to mansplain something to me. I'm done."

# My Body Is Ready

Though this sentence can also be used as a term of endearment (as in, "my body is ready for your body to be on and/or around my body"), it can also be appropriate when talking about something you're really stoked about. It often accompanies a photo or GIF of someone posing seductively (or creepily). Reggie Fils-Aime (the president and COO of Nintendo of America and also a major a bad-ass) coined the phrase in 2007, when he said, "My body...my body is ready," before stepping onto a WiiFit Balance Board at an E3 Press Conference.

EXAMPLE: "*Once Upon a Time* got renewed for another season! My body is ready." "My fave fic author posted a new chapter! My body is ready." "A new *Zelda* game was just announced!" "My body is Reggie." (Get it? Because Nintendo!)

# OTP

That special romantic character pairing that pulls at your heart-strings and floods you with feels in a way that none of the others do? That's your one true pairing, or OTP. If you feel like you might have a few OTPs, you can rank them as OTP1, OTP2, OTP3, and so on. You may also have a BROTP, your favorite-ever nonromantic besties—thus, "bros" (*Psych* fans, I'm looking at you). If there's a pairing you absolutely can't stand and would never, ever support, that's a NOTP. And you don't have to limit your favorite ship to two characters—if there's a third involved, they can be your OT3.

EXAMPLE: "Sam Carter and Jack O'Neill from *Stargate SG-1* are my forever OTP, so Sam and Pete Shanahan are definitely a NOTP." "Natasha Romanoff and Steve Rogers are adorbs together as friends, but I'd never ship them—total BROTP."

# Shipping

"Shipping" is taken from the word "relationship," and it describes both a romantic pairing and the act of really, really wanting two people to kiss/be together forever/have lots of sex all the time. Typically, fangirls ship fictional characters, but we have been known to ship IRL people, too. Ship wars—when shippers of conflicting ships get into heated arguments—are common in fandom but should be avoided. We can all get along.

EXAMPLE: "I totally ship Kirk/Spock and Mulder/Scully, but the Minerva McGonagall/Tom Riddle ship kind of squicks me out."

# Ship Names

In much the same way that terrible gossip magazines do for real-life couples, fangirls traditionally create one-word names for ship pairings. Ship names are frequently a portmanteau of the characters' names (e.g., Spike + Buffy = Spuffy) but can also be something unusual and idiosyncratic that only people within that particular fan community are familiar with.

EXAMPLES: Caskett (Castle/Beckett from *Castle*), Pepperony (Pepper Potts/Tony Stark from *Iron Man*), Whouffle (The Eleventh Doctor/Clara from *Doctor Who*), Doccubus (Lauren/Bo from *Lost Girl*), Peeniss (Katniss/Peeta from *The Hunger Games*. I just), and Wincest (Sam/Dean from *Supernatural*—I don't judge).

# Spoiler

A spoiler is any information about a story, plotline, or character that is revealed ahead of time. (That thing where you go on Twitter and read about how everyone dies at the end of issue #27 and then you rage forever because *how dare someone reveal that*? That's a spoiler.) Since no one wants the ending of something ruined on the Internet before she gets the chance to read, watch, or play it, posting sensitive info with a spoiler alert is good form—it's like putting up a handy DO NOT ENTER sign for those late to the bandwagon. Along with strategically placed blog jumps to hide spoilery GIFs behind a cut, this is your way of respecting other geek girls' feels.

EXAMPLE: "Spoiler alert: Everyone you love on *Game of Thrones* is probably going to die."

# Squee

The universal noise of the fangirl, the squee is a high-pitched, often involuntary sound emitted when something is just so awesome and amazing you can't control yourself. Internet lore says it derives from a portmanteau of "squeal" and "glee," but more likely it's just a fun things to say. (By the way, squee is in the Oxford English Dictionary; it's a verb defined as "used to express great delight or excitement" and can be conjugated as "squees," "squeeing," or "squeed.")

EXAMPLE: "My OTP just became canon! *Squeeeeee!*" "Jensen Ackles asked if he could grab my butt during a photo op! *Squeeeeeeeeeee!*"

# Stan/Stanning

"Stan" is a portmanteau of "stalker" and "fan," and it designates a particularly hardcore, majorly obsessed fan of one particular thing (and *that's totally okay*, we are here for you, girl). If you're actively stanning for a celeb, you might have a Tumblr dedicated to reblogging GIFs of their butt, or you might buy twelve copies of their newest album, or you might spam hatesites with a bunch of photos where your celeb true love looks incredibly attractive. Just remember: a good stan is a respectful stan. Everyone can love what they love.

**EXAMPLE:** I stan Sebastian Stan, because stanning for Stan is the best way to be a stan.

# Terms of Endearment

Fangirls never settle for saying things like "I'm really into Charlie Day right now" or "Tricia Helfer could totally get it." We express our affection for celebrities and fictional characters by calling them names, asking rhetorical questions, issuing commands, or just…making sounds. It might seem like you're saying horrible things about the person you love, but no. You're just expressing your feels in the best way possible—honestly.

**EXAMPLES:** "Life ruiner!" "What are you?" "Ugh what an actual jerk," "Can you not," "Bye ovaries," "stahp," "hnng," "UNF."

# This.

For when "I agree with what was just said" is too many words. Even more than a like, a reblog, or a favorite, *this* is a handy one-syllable reaction that shows not only do you concur, but you are also putting in the effort to say so in a separate comment. Can also be repeated ad nauseam, for effect (i.e., *thisthisthisthissssss*).

**EXAMPLE:** "Going to see movies made by female writers or directors is super important." "THIS."

# TW and CW

Short for "trigger warning" and "content warning," these tags let you know if text, images, or videos within a post could cause a negative response in some readers. Trigger warnings are often used for posts about potentially emotionally harmful topics like abuse, eating disorders, or self-harm. Content warnings are similar to trigger warnings but usually are used in a broader sense. Both indicate content that a reader may want to avoid depending on her personal triggers. Everyone's triggers are different, based on past experiences. The best way to use these warnings on Tumblr is in the tags, like this: "self-harm tw" or "pregnancy cw." If you're posting an article on Twitter or Facebook that you think is likely to affect someone, you can put a warning in the text preceding your link.

EXAMPLE: Here's a piece I wrote about negative relationship role models for young girls in the media. Trigger warning for abuse. #abuse tw

# Resistance Is Futile: Converting Your Friends to Fangirls

Trust: I know how hard it is not to just freak out *all the time* about your current obsession. But flailing, squeezing, and swooning *all the time* can scare off the uninitiated.

Here's a true and entirely embarrassing story: I met a girl named Karyn in the seventh grade (in Library Club, whatever) and immediately decided we had to be best friends. Because at age twelve (and still at age twenty-five, really) I was really good at being a huge nerd, and pretty terrible at socializing, I went about gaining her friendship the only way I knew how: inviting her over to my house and forcing her to watch eight straight hours of *Stargate SG-1*. While my plan ultimately worked and we remain besties to this day, I do *not* recommend this method for gaining or creating new fangirl friends. Here are a few other, *good* ways to win friends to your fandom.

## Ease into it.

If you want to get your bud into, say, *Supernatural*, don't open by casually mentioning that it's been on the air for a *decade*. Instead, start by sending her funny GIFs or talking about amazing moments from the show, and then sit down and watch the pilot together (and maybe a couple more episodes, just to get her good and hooked). If you want to get her into a game and she's just not a gamer, start off slow with something easy and recognizable, like a Nintendo game. The Mario gang is culturally ubiquitous, and many of their games are chill multiplayer jams with no real consequences (like *Mario Kart* or *Super Smash Bros.*). No matter what, keep things breezy and fun. Once you've gotten past her "I don't really watch TV/game/read comics" roadblock, then you can heap on the praise for your faves.

## Play human recommendation engine.

Relate whatever you like to something she likes. I once sold a friend on *Borderlands* by telling her it was like a *Firefly* expanded universe simulator (it is). If your friend is into novels and you want to share your love of comics, give her a few trades of something wordy, like *Y: The Last Man*. If she's totally in love with Sherlock and *Kill Bill*, get her the first season of *Elementary* on DVD and bask together in the glory that is Lucy Liu's Joan Watson.

## Discover something together.

Finding fierce passion for a new fandom is way more fun when you have someone to fangirl with. Grab one of your friends and pledge to wait to watch something until you can watch it together. Invite her over, microwave some popcorn, and make a day of it. Not only will the show be more fun, but you and your friend will have something to bond over forever—you'll always share that fandom (which also makes birthdays and general gift-giving a lot easier!). Even if you're long-distance Internet friends, call each other up on Skype, count down, and start the episode simultaneously. You can give concurrent commentary from miles away, and you'll be able to freak out together as soon as the episode ends!

## Make it a party.

You don't have to limit your fangirling to one friend, of course. Make your marathon into a mind-blowing megabash by inviting a bunch of friends to experience the awesome together. They don't have to be hard-core fangirls; in fact, it's cool if you can all start from the beginning and make your way through a show together. Pick a day when everyone is free, commit to a certain number of episodes, and get going on the marathon. You won't be able to talk about anything else for weeks, and you'll be the awesomest group of friends ever. By the way, make sure every girl brings some sort of snack item to the party. Essential.

# Give the gift of fandom.

If you can't experience a new fandom with your friends, it's always a great idea to send them something you're sure they'll love. One year, for friends' birthdays I gave the first *Rat Queens* trade paperback, the original *Dragon Age* game, and the first season of *Life on Mars*. You already know how obsessed you are with these things, and you know your friends pretty well, so you're probably the best judge of who would be into what. And the best part is, once they love it, they're going to be grateful to you forever. *Forever.* Use that power wisely.

# Don't get defensive.

If your fangirling freaks your friends out, don't fret. Remind them (and yourself!) that throughout history, the best kinds of literature—the ones that have survived the longest—are the books that touch people on a *human* level. Your fandoms are like that: fiction, no matter the form, allows you to live a thousand meaningful experiences and relationships that you could never have in real life. Getting invested in a fictional world means you have a wonderful imagination, a big heart, and the capacity for endless creativity. No one can say anything bad about that.

# Fangirling IRL: Where to Go to Find Your People

We lady nerds have a reputation for being shy, at least in person. (The Internet's a whole 'nother story.) But it turns out it's way easy to find like-minded friends if you venture beyond your university residence, workplace, etc., and into the world of geeky social events. Not only will you be doing an activity you already love, but meeting people at nerdy get-togethers also guarantees that—even if they're really into *Kill La Kill* and you're more of a *Sailor Moon* kind of gal— they will at least understand your passion for nerdery. And hey, you might even be able to convert some people to your particular fandom, or vice versa. Here are a few of the best places to team up.

## Your Local Comic Book Store

Besides being an excellent place to shop for the latest *Ms. Marvel*, your local comic book store is a great home base to use as you start seeking out geeky social events. They might have a bulletin board where people can post about upcoming fun-times or a spot near the registers for folks to leave flyers.

Even if you're not into comics, that's okay—comics stores are usually supportive of the entire local geek community. You might find they sell tickets for nerdy burlesque shows, advertise about geek-themed comedy nights, or host screenings of locally created webseries. Don't forget to stop by on Wednesdays, which are New Comic Book Day, when everyone hits the shop to pick up the newest issues. Head over and ask a friendly-lookin' fangirl at the stacks what's good. Now you've got a new friend and new things to read! (If you don't have a comics-specific shop near you, you can do the same in any bookseller. Just head to the graphic novel, fantasy, or sci-fi section.) If you're more of a gamer than a comic book girl, trek over to your closest game shop on Tuesdays—that's when new games always release. And remember, if any sales clerk makes you feel unwelcome, don't stand for it! Report the incident to a manager, or take your dollars elsewhere.

FIND ONE NEAR YOU: The best place to look is The-Master-List.com and FindAComicShop.com, both huge directories of every comic book and trading card store in the United States and Canada.

# Midnight Movies

Anyone who shows up for a midnight opening-night screening of the latest, shiniest geek flick must be a diehard nerd. I mean, you'd *have* to be a killer-huge fan to wait in line for hours for the newest *Star Wars* or Marvel Universe film, right?

Good thing waiting in line is a great place to make friends: chat, compare costumes, or bring a game like *Cards Against Humanity* to pass the time, and everyone around you will instantly love you. Sometimes smaller theaters hold special advance screenings for blockbusters and you can grab tickets on the cheap, plus they usually offer fun events to draw you away from the big chains (e.g., costume contests, pre-movie video games on the big screen, trivia, etc.).

Also, check out the indie theaters in your town. You might find local Browncoats hosting a Can't Stop the Serenity event or a revival screening of your fave old-school flick (*Gremlins* fan meetup, anyone?).

FIND ONE NEAR YOU: Moviefone and Fandango in the United States and Cineplex in Canada are solid resources but don't neglect your area's small chain, indie, or alt theaters to find the craziest midnight screenings—check out indiefilmpage.com to find one nearby.

# Makerspaces

If you're into programming, messing with tech stuff, or any kind of DIY, you should check out your local makerspace. Also known as a hackerspace, hacklab, TechShop, or fab lab, these all share the same deal: a community-operated workspace where you can collaborate and socialize with people who love the same stuff.

Hackerspaces are usually found in and around university campuses, community centers, and info shops and are great for the development of open-source software, new hardware, and electronic art. Makerspaces tend to focus on stuff like 3D printing, alternative media, and building any kind of crazy contraptions you could possibly imagine. The spaces typically come fully stocked with tools, rad machines, game consoles, crafting supplies, and raw materials you might not be able to get your hands on yourself. Best of all, you'll be meeting and working with other like-minded hackers and makers in your area.

FIND ONE NEAR YOU: Makerspace.com has a worldwide directory of every makerspace, tool library, and library workspace across the globe. Hackerspaces.meetup.com and Hackerspaces.org also have huge global directories.

# Zombie Walks

Why limit your excellent costume to Halloween when you can take it out for another shamble? Get together with other undead divas in all your groaning glory. Everyone's out to have a great time at a zombie walk, so it's easy to introduce yourself to another gang of gnarly-looking walkers and ask if you can join forces.

If you're not sure how to put together a great zombie look, don't fall to the ground moaning "*brraaaaaiiiinnns*" in despair; it's super easy. For that rotting air, use lash glue to create realistic-looking gashes that you can dust with red and brown makeup (eyeshadow works great); try using food coloring to tint clear detergent red for easy-to-clean "blood." When the zombie walk is over, toss your outfit in the wash with some regular detergent, and it'll come out as good as new. Dead serious.

FIND ONE NEAR YOU: The ZombieWalk.com forums have threads for every U.S. state as well as tons of other countries, as do the listings at CrawloftheDead.com.

# Board Game Cafés, Barcades, or Any Establishment with Fun and Games

Nothing goes together better than food, friends, and intense gaming competition. For caffeinated daytime fun, grab a couple friends, buy a cappuccino, and settle at a board game café, where you can hang out (some let you stay all day, some charge by the hour) and take your pick from an incredible selection of tabletop games. For a boozy good time in the evening, hit up a barcade, a nightspot that's puntastically exactly what it sounds like—a bar with a ton of old-school coin-operated pinball and arcade cabinets (I'd bet my quarters there's one near you).

Either way, you're guaranteed to have a blast. Chug chai tea and best your besties at Monopoly, or bring it back to the '80s Dazzler-style by having a few beers while you aggressively button-smash over an infuriatingly difficult level of *Burger Time* or *Galaga*. Find yourself a few people short? Team up with another group of gamers and make insta-friends! If board game cafés and barcades haven't yet reached your neighborhood, chances are you do have a comic book store, bookseller, or hobby shop that hosts a game night where you can take part in some Munchkin, Magic, or Yu-Gi-Oh! action.

**FIND ONE NEAR YOU:** Check out gaming clubs on meetup.com, or Google [your town name] + "board game café" or "barcade." Easy!

## Comics Classes and Game Jams

If you want to try to infiltrate your local comics or game creator community, there's a couple different places you should check out *stat*. The art and design department at the college in your town is a great place to start. Even if you can't or don't want to enroll, you can audit a few game design courses or seminars like "How to Draw for Comics." You should also check for game jams or comic jams in your area. Those are nights when creators get together, sit around (potentially over drinks), and just code or draw while keeping one another company. These might be independently run or hosted by organizations like Dames Making Games. They'll be full of people you'll want to know (and who will want to know you, too!).

**FIND ONE NEAR YOU:** Hit up the online class directory of your local art school, community college, or university and see what classes are available for auditing. For game jams, check out Compohub .net and GameJamCentral.com.

## Pub Trivia Nights

Pub trivia is the perfect place to trot out all your geeky facts, have a couple drinks (alcoholic or non), and make some new friends in the process. (In my city, we have a monthly Geek Trivia night run by Stephanie Cooke, intrepid assistant to *Fables* creator Bill Willingham, that brings out tons of geeks from around town.)

The best part of trivia nights is that you don't have to come as part of a team; in fact, showing up alone is often way cooler because you get to integrate yourself into a table of new, nerdy, knowledgeable friends. I went to my very first pub trivia night by myself, terrified, and certain I was going to embarrass myself beyond recovery. But, with the exception of the one dude who asked me to "prove that I read comics" by naming Peter Parker's birth parents (Richard and Mary, for the record), everyone else was incredibly welcoming, kind, and like-minded. In my experience, geeks are always so stoked to find other awesome geeks in the wild that you will instantly find yourself surrounded by new besties. Even if you arrive with a pal or two, team up with strangers—aka future friends—and smoke the competition.

FIND ONE NEAR YOU: Keep tabs on local pubs to see if any throw trivia nights. Many will post on Twitter or Instagram the day of.

# Renaissance Faires

If you dream of living the *Dungeons and Dragons* life full-time, or wish you could swashbuckle the seven seas in your fab new corset, a Renaissance, Medieval, or Pirate Faire is the place for you. Usually held in summer or early fall, faires welcome lovable weirdos of all types (costumes aren't usually mandatory, but are highly recommended!) for jousts, dances, live music, magic shows, and—of course—flagons of ale and giant turkey legs. Most faires employ a cast of fully dressed professional actors who stroll the grounds talking in Ye Olde English, but they don't mind winking at historical accuracy, either. So don't be surprised if you see Queen Elizabeth taking selfies with a steampunk fairy princess, or the Three Musketeers crossing swords with someone dressed as the Tenth Doctor.

FIND ONE NEAR YOU: TheRenList.com, RenaissanceMagazine.com, and RenFaire.com all have tons of Faire listings. Wikipedia (of course!) has a super-comprehensive list of Faires at en.wikipedia.org/wiki/List_of_ Renaissance_fairs.

# Blog Meetups

Chances are—unless you're into some seriously niche fandoms—you are not the only person who frequents, faves, and comments on the blogs you read. And some of your fellow fans might live near you! You might also catch wind of a local gathering on Twitter (a tweetup!) or on a forum that you frequent. Nothing is better than getting together with a bunch of gals and giggling about the latest goofs on the interwebs, trust.

FIND ONE NEAR YOU: Keep an eye out for announcements from the blog webmistress about meetups, and offer to set one up in your area if no one has yet. Ask around—there may be a satellite Facebook group where people set up IRL events.

# Book Clubs

Forget your mom's wine-and-kvetch-fests. Book clubs are totally dope—like English class if you were allowed to read only books that you actually like *and* snack and sip while discussing them. Don't limit yourself to the latest Oprah-approved best seller. These days, book clubs discuss everything from graphic novels to the latest in dystopian YA lit.

FIND ONE NEAR YOU: Local indie bookstores and libraries are always a good start. If you're into YA, visit ForeverYoungAdult.com to find a local chapter of snarky lady readers.

# Burlesque Shows

Burlesque is the dream combo of babely ladies, body positivity, and bubbly nerdery. Anyone is welcome in the burlesque world, regardless of size, shape, or gender, which means performances are always diverse and wonderful. Shows often have a theme, and for some reason a lot of burlesque performers also happen to be huge nerds, so the themes are in line with what we already love. (The best burlesque performances I've ever seen were Poisonne's performance as the sexily evil GLaDOS, from *Portal*, and Barely Legal Leelando's boylesque as the Joker. YouTube them!) Go, enjoy some empowerment, and get your nerd on. Simultaneously!

FIND ONE NEAR YOU: BurlesqueBaby.blogspot.com and RedHot Annie.com have directories of burlesque performers according to their area in the United States and Canada. PinUpAmerica.com has a comprehensive list of performers across the United States.

# LARPing and Quidditch Games

Live Action Role-Playing—aka LARPing—is like playing your favorite RPG IRL, or tabletop gaming where the tabletop is an open field and *you're* the minifig. Spend an afternoon casting spells, dueling with foam weapons, and rocking a cool costume as you and your fellow geeks fight battles and puzzle out scenarios written up by your local gamemaster. More of a contact-sports fan? Try out for a team of Muggle Quidditch, a (sadly) nonflying version of Harry Potter's favorite game that's played in leagues worldwide. Run fast to catch the snitch (a neutral athlete in yellow). And don't worry: the bludgers are just dodgeballs.

FIND ONE NEAR YOU: Check out the LARP list at Larping.org to find a live-action RP group—the map tool makes searching easy. The International Quidditch Association (yes, it's real!) has links to leagues in many countries at iqaquidditch.org.

# Create Your Own

None of the events in your area tickle your exact fancy? Or maybe you live in a small town where not much geeky stuff happens?

Major bummer, but you know who can change that? *You*, girl. It might seem daunting, but creating your own specifically themed nerdy event is your ticket to meeting people with your same crazy-intense interest. (My favorite-ever in-person geek event? The double-bill *Dr. Horrible/Buffy* musical sing-along screening that a group of Joss fans held in the back of a local bar.)

If you're interested in setting up your own event, start by figuring out what you're trying to set up—a trivia night? a tabletop gaming event?—and gauge interest by posting about it on social media. Next, look into local comics stores, bookstores, or libraries that have space for community use. Or ask around at pubs—some might let you rent out the space for cheap or even use it for free, so long as everyone who shows up buys something to eat or drink. Once your idea and venue are locked down, advertise online and leave flyers at cafés, bars, and other nerdy hangouts. Then have a blast! I guarantee that your Browncoat Trivia Night will make you the hero of every Whedonite within a hundred-mile radius. (You can thank me later.)

Thinking even *bigger*? The ultimate geek-girl gathering is, of course, the convention! Find out more about cons starting on page 104.

# Let Your Geek Flag Fly: Bringing Fandom into Your "Normal" Life

Finding nerdy friends clearly isn't enough for us fangirls. We need to express our nerdiness in real life, in as many ways as is humanly possible. We're not always loud about it, but we're definitely proud. Here are some (sorta) subtle ways to incorporate the stuff you love into the way you live.

## Everyday Cosplay

FANDOM LEVEL: n00b

Although I might not recommend rocking full cosplay on a daily basis (your Zelda gown probably doesn't fit your work dress code, sadly), you can definitely show your stuff in a "societally" acceptable way. Jewelry is always a good option. Try Rebel Alliance earrings, a Triforce brooch, or a Companion Cube ring to flash small symbols that a Muggle probably won't notice. You can find great geeky bling at local boutiques, at vendor booths at your next convention, or online (tons of which you can find in this book's resources section, page 197). The same goes for accessories. An N7 bag or decoupage comic-book heels will look cute with any professional or academic outfit. If you're heading to an event or even just out for the weekend, you might want to take things a bit further—rock a cute TARDIS tank dress or your best Corellian Bloodstripe leggings. And remember, buying a T-shirt from your fave indie webcomic doesn't just look awesome, it also gives precious, precious money to an artist you love. Yay!

# Customize Your Space

Fangirlizing your space is fully customizable, depending on your living sitch, cash flow, and dedication to interior design. Posters and collages are fangirl classics that will never go out of style, and a *Sherlock* collage or Batman cork board will bring life to any old boring wall. If you don't want to go the DIY route, you can find amazing original art online or by visiting Artist Alleys at conventions. Either way, make sure your one-of-a-kind piece doesn't get crushed. Hit up a craft store for some cheap frames, or head to an art shop for the professional treatment.

Another good decor option is the collect-and-display route: grab a bunch of affordable snap-together bookshelves and use them to show off all your sweet figurines and collectables. And if that's *still* not enough for you, go full-on fantasy and design your

entire space based on the fandom of your choice. (A friend of mine visits antiques shops religiously in an attempt to put together a living room that looks as much like the Gryffindor Common Room as possible, right down to the tapestries.) If you're artistic, or have artsy friends, try sketching and painting a mural right on your wall or a smaller saying above a door ("Speak, friend, and enter," perhaps?). Peel-and-stick removable vinyl wall decals that you can grab on Etsy are wicked for this, too, and make for a less permanent option if your folks or landlords prefer carry-and-go artwork.

# Host a Killer Prerelease Party

FANDOM LEVEL: n00b

What better way to welcome a long-awaited book, movie, or game than with a huge nerd-bash? Whether it's in your own space or over at a friend's, fully theme your party night to match whatever event you're headed to later (which will probably involve a line for some midnight release). You'll need to get DIY with the decorations to make your party feel like you're in your fave fictional world.

If you're throwing a *Harry Potter* themed bash, say, for the premiere of *Fantastic Beasts and Where to Find Them*, then you could hang some (unlit) candles from the ceiling with clear fishing wire, deck out some tables in the four house colors, throw some stuffed owls around, and hang big swaths of discount-bin fabric onto the walls like tapestries. If you've got a big tree in your yard, stake a sign in front that says "Whomping Willow—do not touch."

Next, get some food and whip up baked goods (if baked goods aren't at your party, I don't want to be invited) that match your theme. For our dream Potter party, there are a million easy-to-follow recipes online for re-creating the entirety of Honeydukes Sweet Shop, from licorice wands to cockroach clusters (that'd be melted chocolate over broken pretzels, obv). For music, grab the soundtrack to a previously released game or movie in the series (you can never go wrong with "Hedwig's Theme"). Finally: *costumes*. Make dressing up mandatory (silly, slapdash, and thrown together is okay!), and you will have the best-looking group of fangirls around. Keep your costumes on when you head out to the event and you'll be the envy of every fangirl there.

# Craft Up a Storm

FANDOM LEVEL: Intermediate

Combine your skillsets, nerdgirls! If you love to knit, crochet, cross-stitch, sew, iron-on, decoupage, solder, make salt art, *whatever*, you can use what life rolled you to make the geekiest goodies ever. Rupee-shaped soap bars, Ramona Flowers star purses, cross-stitches of the One Direction boys—you can make anything your geeky heart desires. The best part about geeky crafting (besides personal satisfaction) is that there's a huge market for it! Once you're happy with your work and feeling industrious, set up a shop on Etsy and share your nerdy creations with the whole wide world. You'll be making spare cash for cons in no time.

# Study Up

FANDOM LEVEL: Intermediate

If you're a student, your nerdery doesn't have to be just a pastime—it can become your academic focus! More colleges and universities are treating geek stuff as Srs Bsns and offering classes that explore, examine, and critique the books, movies, and TV shows we love. There are classes on zombies in popular media (Columbia College), Star Trek and religion (Indiana University), the science of superheroes (University of California–Irvine), and even Tolkien's Elvish (University of Wisconsin). Check your course catalog (the Media Studies department is a good place to start) and see what strikes your fancy. Or, if you have a project in mind (like compiling an oral history of a particular fandom), talk to a favorite professor and see if she'll sponsor an independent study. You'd be surprised how many academic types are secretly fangirls, too!

# Start a Tribute Band

FANDOM LEVEL: Intermediate

If you're musically inclined, grab some of your nerdy band bros and start singing and jamming. Whether you decide to perform straight-up covers of the *Star Wars* cantina theme, want to make some wizard rock about your love for Lucius Malfoy, re-create your favorite filk tune, or beep-boop out some chiptune versions of hit songs, a geek band is a great way to get out your fandom feels.

Don't fret if you're more band geek than punk rocker. How cool would a string quartet cover of "Still Alive" sound, amirite? And don't forget to give your group an appropriately nerdy name (puns are a plus). If you're looking for musical inspiration, check out folks like the Doubleclicks (two gals who sing about ladies in geekery), Marian Call (a singer-songwriter with lots of amazing tunes inspired by *Firefly*), and Malukah and Rebecca Mayes Muses, both of whom make songs inspired by their fave video games.

# Get a Geeky Tattoo

FANDOM LEVEL: Hardcore

It's the ultimate way to show your lifelong dedication to a fandom—permanently inking it on your body! I think geeky tattoos are a brilliant idea for the devoted fangirl, which would probably be why I have two (a wrought-iron Deathly Hallows symbol on my ribs, and a *Mass Effect* Spectre symbol on my forearm). But it's an important and forever-times decision, so here are a few things you might want to keep in mind before you take the plunge:

- Research all the great artists in your area (try Yelp, Tumblrs like SorryYouRuinedYourself, reddit.com/r/tattoos, or recommendations from friends) until you find one whose portfolio jives with your style. If they're expensive, that probably means their work is good. This is going to be on your body forever, so it's worth saving up for.

- Your design will be a collaboration between you and the tattoo artist, so let your artist make the art. Never steal other people's designs from the Internet—it's considered rude at best and art theft at worst. Bring images of things you admire, and ask your artist to use them as inspiration. You're going to end up with completely original artwork designed just for you, your taste, and your body.

- Don't ever get an in-home or "stick and poke" tattoo. They're dangerous and never look as good as professional ink. Save your cash for something pretty *and* safe.

- If it's your first-ever tattoo, consider starting with a location that's easy to cover, like feet, upper arms, or ribs. That way, you can figure out whether you like having a tattoo without greater consequences. Neck, hand, and finger tattoos really should be left until you're sure the look is for you.

- If you're tattooing your arms, make sure the imagery isn't upside down. The design should face toward your hands so that when your arms are hanging at your side, the image is right side up.

- Be sure to double, triple, and quadruple check the spelling of any text before you get inked, especially if the text is in a foreign language.

- Don't get a tattoo just for the sake of getting a tattoo. Tons of fangirls want ink the second they turn eighteen just because they can (and because they want to carry a drawing of their OTP wherever they go). Before making an appointment, it's better to wait until an image or an idea really speaks to you, even if all it says is "I'm super pretty!" Tattoos don't need to have some deep meaning behind them. Still, life is long, and (not to sound like your mom) tattoos are permanent.

Interviews with

Jill Pantozzi,

Jane Espenson,

Erin Morgenstern,

and Tara Platt

# JILL PANTOZZI

◇ ◇ ◇

editor in chief of the Mary Sue

@JillPantozzi

## What does the word "fangirl" mean to you?

Fangirl, just like "geek girl," "nerd girl," etc., means someone who is extra passionate about what they love. We're all fans of something, but being a fangirl means you're willing to show it, unabashedly and with great vigor.

## How has being a geek positively influenced your life?

Being a geek has made me who I am today. I never would have guessed it as a young girl in the sixth grade, finding another student in school who also loved *Star Trek: The Next Generation*, that simply loving what I love would eventually lead me down the path of my current career. And I couldn't be more thrilled about it. The saying is "love what you do and you'll never work a day in your life." I do love what I do, but I also work very hard, and the results have made me a very happy adult. Not just that, but I wouldn't trade the friends I've made simply because I'm a geek for anything in the world.

## What advice can you give geek girls for their careers or personal lives?

Don't change your opinion just because others don't agree with it, but don't be afraid to change because you want to.

# JANE ESPENSON

◇ ❖ ◇

TV writer and producer for
shows you may have heard of
like *Buffy*, *Battlestar Galactica*,
*Torchwood*, *Husbands*, and
*Once Upon a Time*, nerd hero

@JaneEspenson

### What does the word "fangirl" mean to you?

Personally, I've never really noticed a gender-based difference in how fans react to their favorite shows and the people involved in them. I'd say a fangirl or fanboy is someone who has found a property that has resonated so much with their personal life that they find joy in contact with almost everything associated with it. It's a joyful thing to be.

### How has being a geek positively influenced your life?

Oh, that's easy. My very first TV opportunity was through *Star Trek: The Next Generation*. If I hadn't known and adored that show, I would not have been able to take advantage of that opportunity.

### What advice can you give geek girls for their careers or personal lives?

Get creative, get original, get ambitous. Study your craft—create the best costumes, best fic, whatever. And, I'd suggest, don't stop there. Look for ways to go beyond what others are doing. Make original worlds of your own, adapt your fic and publish it, find a way to market your creations, or whatever. Look into ways to turn what you love into something that can become a support to you in more ways than one. I wasn't content with watching shows—I was itching to get behind the scenes and found a way to do it. You can take whatever you love about fandom and turn it into something original that starts with you.

# ERIN MORGENSTERN

◇ ◇ ◇

writer, artist, and author of the
super-popular award-winning
fantasy novel *The Night Circus*

@erinmorgenstern

### What does the word "fangirl" mean to you?

I think of a "fangirl" as a leveled-up regular fan. I regard it as a gender-neutral term and often use it as a verb.

### How has being a geek positively influenced your life?

I'm shy, so sharing geeky interests helps me immensely with meeting people and making friends. It gives you a common language, and for easily tongue-tied people like me, that can be invaluable.

And being friends with other geek-speaking people often results in finding new geeky interests. My husband got me into video games. I knew we were meant to be when we got through all of the cooperative levels of *Portal 2* without a single disagreement. (Being a geek has also been very good for my career, parts of *The Night Circus* are odes to fandom.)

### What advice can you give geek girls for their careers or personal lives?

Love what you love and don't be afraid to try new things.

I think sometimes there's an expectation that if you're a geek girl, you're supposed to love x, y, and *Doctor Who*, but if you don't, that's okay. The geek umbrella covers such a wide expanse of interests, trust your own tastes when it comes to figuring out which ones are right for your unique flavor of geek.

# TARA PLATT

◇ ◇ ◇

actress, author, producer, and voice-over artist for countless anime and video games, including Naruto (Temari) and League of Legends (Katarina)

@taraplatt

### What does the word "fangirl" mean to you?

I think fangirl, or any fandom, is really about showing your love and passion for something. I fangirl-out over math—physics, in particular—and numbers. That brings me joy and a giddy feeling. Thankfully, we live in an amazing world where any number of topics of interest, from comics to movies to sports to arts and sciences, bring out fans who can participate and join forces in appreciating them.

### How has being a geek positively influenced your life?

Well, it is a fun little corner of the world where there seems to be acceptance for who and what you are. People are intrinsically searching for who they want to be in the world, and it seems that geekdom has become a haven for striving for your best.

### What advice can you give geek girls for their careers or personal lives?

Be willing to put forth your best version of yourself and don't let anyone else's interpretation of who they think you are get in the way of you being you.

# chapter two

# [Fandom Intensifies]: Geek Girls Online

The Internet's a vast and magical realm. And it's a great place for fangirls worldwide to form long-lasting friendships. But sadly, it's not all Rainbow Dash and unicorns. There's improper tagging and fandom fights and the icky, cave-dwelling, grotesque trolls that feed on the power of online anonymity. But never fear, fangirls! Get your crossbows and capes ready because we're boldly going out into teh intarnetz.

# The Seven Kingdoms of the Internet

Gone are the days when fangirls had to seek out obscure usenet groups, IRC channels, and janky all-caps WEB PAGES (miss u, Geocities) to hang out with their people. Everyone and their mother is on social media these days (love u, @NancyMaggs!), but that doesn't make it easy to venture forth. Different social media sites are good for different things, and all have rules about stuff like where#to #put #those hashtags# and how to stay safe. Ladies, everyone is a n00b once. Allow me to present you with this handy worldmap of Internet etiquette (internetiquette? /groan) and safety.

## Key

**Kingdom:** The website in question

**Currency:** What sort of stuff you can share

**Terrain:** The lay of the land—the site's main interface

## Kingdom: Twitter

CURRENCY: 140-character (or under!) text posts

TERRAIN: Timeline (or tweet stream, or Twitter feed)

Twitter is fantastic for all sorts of reasons. You can keep tabs on your fave celebs, shows, and news outlets as they send out bite-sized blips on the regular; you can build a list of your IRL buddies to follow; you can discover fellow fangirls who love #GameofThrones; or you can do all three. You don't have to use your real name—it's not Facebook, nobody cares—but many people do, and that's where Twitter gets really rad. It's an incredible resource for making connections with likeminded gals, meeting friends, and even professional networking.

- ➢ Live-tweeting (posting your reactions to a live event as it happens) is a great way to share and connect. Do it for TV shows, con panels, release parties, whatever you love, and the rest of us will live vicariously.

- ➢ Spamming is the worst! Unless you're live-tweeting an event of nerd importance, try to hold back a little. Twitter will briefly jail your account (i.e., freeze you from posting new tweets) if you fire out too many missives at once, so keep it together.

- ➢ Now that Twitter auto-displays images, avoid posting NSFW pics with the Twitter photo uploader. Some people use Twitter at work, in coffee shops, or at their parents' house. Squick! Post an NSFW warning and link to an outside image (rather than uploading it to Twitter) instead.

- ➢ Nobody trusts egg people. If you still have the default image as your profile photo, you will not make any friends! You don't have to put up your actual lovely face, but at least swap in something that shows you're human (like your favorite Miyazaki heroine, say).

- ➢ You don't have to share your tweets with everyone. You can "protect" your account so that only people you approve can follow you and see what you tweet. If you do want a public profile, be sure to change your settings so that Twitter doesn't automatically add a location. You never know who might want to find you in the world, so better safe than sorry.

- Keep your account safe from tweetjackers by enabling two-step login verification (you'll use your phone to verify that it's really you). You can also require personal information (like your phone number) to request a password reset.

- It's great to tweet a picture of the line at the midnight premiere you're attending or the geeky sign that someone put up outside your fave coffee shop, but be wary—even with the "add location" option turned off, those kinds of photos can give away exactly where you are. If you do want to tweet location-specific stuff, wait until you've moved on to your next hangout.

- Following someone who's constantly spamming your feed with "hilarious" RTs or just too many random thoughts? You can turn off retweets for certain accounts (so you see only things they post themselves) or "mute" them to avoid seeing their tweets at all (but still appear on their followers list). No hurt feelings!

 ## Kingdom: Facebook

CURRENCY: Status updates, pictures, links, videos … almost anything you can copy/paste into that "what's happening?" box

TERRAIN: News feed

You probably know how to use Facebook with your real name to stay in touch with family and people from your real-life past (helloooo, weird junior prom date!). But if you're a writer, artist, cosplayer, or anyone who wants to show off her cool ~creative stuff~, you can start up a Facebook fan page to grow your following and use it as a marketing platform. This is much less invasive to your personal space. That is, it's okay if complete strangers like your fan page (and it means you won't have to worry about giving them access to your albums from way back in 2007 when you dressed up in a cape and your dad's tie to go see *Order of the Phoenix*).

➢ Invite all your people to like your page—family, friends, folks you went to school with—and encourage them to invite their friends as well. The more shareable content you post (especially photos), the quicker word will spread to new fans. But never feel obligated to friend someone you don't know on your *personal* page. That should be reserved for people you've seen and talked to IRL.

➢ Good Facebook page updates are things that are visual and shareable (as in, a picture of your latest Sakura cosplay or your latest piece of Johnlock fanart). Be sure to stick a little watermark on the image, including a link to your fan page, so that they're identifiable when they circulate outside Facebook. Articles or blog posts your fans might enjoy are always a good bet, too.

➢ If your FB fans want to get in touch and send you stuff, consider renting a post office box near your house. Or get a "virtual" box that will scan and e-mail snail mail letters to you (try virtualpostmail.com)

➢ Like lots of other fan pages! Supporting fangirls and artists is awesome, and it's as easy as a click. If you want to help make their fan count higher without seeing their updates on your news feed all the time, just opt to hide their posts.

➢ Facebook isn't the best place to connect with new people. A friendly message to someone you're not friends with can end up in the black hole of their "other" inbox and never see the light of day. If you ping someone with a PM and they don't re-spond, try getting their attention on another network.

⟫ Don't invite drama. Political debates on Facebook are a never-ending spiral of doom. If someone posts something inflammatory, sexist, or just plain dumb, don't leave a comment (no matter how hilarious and pithy!); defriend or block their updates instead.

 ## Kingdom: Tumblr

CURRENCY: Rebloggable posts—text, photos, quotes, links, chats, audio, or video

TERRAIN: Dashboard

Tumblr is a microblogging platform for curating literally whatever you want: photos, videos, GIFs, text posts, links, whole think pieces—and you definitely don't have to link it to your real identity. I mean, if you want to, that's cool (I do); but you can also make your username castiels-butt-smells-like-delicious-heaven-yum and no one will think any worse of you for it. Tumblr gives you the complete freedom to say or post anything at all. It's also an amazing spot for fandoms and forming fan communities.

⟫ Tag everything you post! This helps other people recognize what they do and don't want to look at. It also helps people find your sweet cosplay, fanfic, or original art. Unlike Twitter, tags on Tumblr can include spaces and punctuation. For exam-ple, I found my amazing iPhone lock screen by searching the hashtag #elementary fanart.

⟫ Get Tumblr Savior. A free add-on for Google Chrome, it allows you to hide posts about any topic. Add the words you want to avoid to your black list (anything from your NOTP pairing to seriously triggering topics), and posts containing them will never again show up on your dash.

> Reblog things you love instead of creating a new post and reposting them. By reblogging, you're giving credit to the original source and adding to that posts' notes, those precious imaginary Internet points we all love.

> Always keep the credit on art. (Imagine spending ages working on a webcomic only to discover it floating around on Tumblr without your name attached! Saddest.) If art has a signature, don't crop it out. If there's a text credit, don't remove it. If you didn't make it, don't credit yourself as the source. Instead, run it through Google image search (click the little camera icon to search with an image) and see if you can track down the original artist's deviantART or Society6 page.

> Don't tag your hate. I can't stress this enough. *Don't tag your hate.* If you're making a post about how terrible you think *Supernatural* is, that's cool (I guess). But do everyone in SuperWhoLock a favor and don't then tag your post #Supernatural.

> If you absolutely must post a spoiler, please tag it, use a jump cut (so that readers have to click to reveal the whole post), or include a *massive* spoiler warning.

> Definitely do browse the themes and find one that you like so that non-Tumblrettes can still enjoy your site as a gorgeous readable blog. But avoid annoying stuff like backgrounds made of GIFs (you could give people seizures!), music that autoplays when people visit your blog (this isn't MySpace), and black backgrounds with neon text (my eyes, my *eyessss*).

# Kingdom: Instagram

**CURRENCY:** Photos, with or without fancy filters, and videos

**TERRAIN:** Feed

Pictures! Pictures everywhere. You can have a personal IG, a cosplay IG, a nail art IG, an IG dedicated to adorable videos of your cat, whatever you want. You can write pretty extensive captions, but every post has to be a photo or video.

‣ If you've got a strong selfie game, bring it to Instagram. Show off your new Iron Man minidress, snap a pic of the loooong line at your next con signing, or just pose whenever you think you're looking supercute. (Though avoid the bathroom selfie. Your toilet is gross.) People might try to make you feel guilty for 'gramming your gorgeous face all the time, but you know what? You feel good about the way you look, and that is always worth sharing.

‣ Make sure you're hashtagging appropriately! This is how people who don't already follow you will find your photos, right? If I'm browsing the #cosplay hashtag, I want to see your stuff, so make sure it's labeled correctly. Other popular tags include #ootd (for your outfit of the day), #TBT and #throwbackthursday (for old-school pictures from your awkward phase—we love you, baby nerdlette!), and #dogsofinstagram and #catsofinstagram (duh).

‣ The IG video time limit is fifteen seconds, which sounds short but is actually a lot of time for a video. Video content is an awesome way to add variety to your IG feed. I especially love artists who shoot themselves sketching and then speed it up. Mesmerizing.

- Supercharge your IG photos with additional apps: extra filters, mirror imaging, grids of multiple pix—you name it, it's out there. Apps like Postagram let you take your stuff offline as postcards and prints, so check those out, too!

- I love all kinds of lady bodies, and I think we should proudly flaunt them to the world. But if you're under eighteen, posting photos of yourself in lingerie can be harmful to your future career or potential relationships; it can even be illegal, depending on the laws where you live. While it's awesome to get a lot of followers or likes for looking hella fab, don't post anything that could come back to haunt you in ten years. (The same goes for photos of underage drinking or any kind of illegal substance!)

- Set your Instagram to "private" if you want to approve everyone who follows you. There's no reason not to, especially if you're worried about safety. But remember, pix on a locked IG account are still, technically, *on the Internet.*

- Just like with Twitter, be careful when posting location-specific pictures if you have a public profile. When in doubt, master the art of the #latergram and put up your sightseeing snaps when you're safely back home.

# Kingdom: Pinterest

CURRENCY: Images

TERRAIN: Boards

Delicious cheesy bread dips? Fabbo *Star Wars* inspired nail art? An endless collection of photos of Natalie Dormer, Lupita Nyong'o, and Emilia Clarke (titled "MY QUEENS," obv) looking fierce as hell?

Pinterest is the online scrapbook of your dreams. Scroll through other users' pins and tack them on your own virtual boards, or grab stuff from wherever you browse the Web with their bookmark bar "Pin It!" button.

➢ You can sign up for Pinterest with your Facebook, Twitter, or Google account info, but only if you're cool with your Real Identity™ being linked with whatever you plan to pin. If you'd prefer to keep your "Lads with Abs" board on the DL, sign up with an e-mail address for relative privacy.

➢ The endless pages of images are a blast to scroll through, but you can also search for anything your heart desires: braiding tips, makeup tutorials, cosplay ideas, whatever. Chances are, someone has pinned it.

➢ Secret boards—aka boards only you can see—are great for whatever you want to keep away from the eyes of Pinterest at large (like all your fave Chris Pine/Zachary Quinto fanart). You can un-secret a secret board, but you can't secret-ify a public board, so think ahead!

➢ Pinterest isn't always great when it comes to crediting original artists, so be a responsible fangirl and try to pin from the artist's homepage whenever you can instead of aggregator sites like WeHeartIt. If anyone clicks through to the art page, you want the artist to get that pageview, like, and/or follow!

 **Kingdom: Reddit**

**CURRENCY:** Upvotes/downvotes on text posts, links, and externally hosted images

**TERRAIN:** Main page, full of topics from your subscribed subreddits

Reddit is both a link aggregator (like Digg) and a kind of hybrid discussion board/news feed. Users can browse links and topics from the default "subreddits," or categories of interest (/r/aww, for example, is only cute animal pictures), or subscribe to (or even create) their own /r/ on any topic they choose.

➤ You don't need a Reddit account to look through most of the offerings, but if you want access to any private or invite-only subs, you'll need a username and mod approval.

➤ Explore the subs! If you're into it, there's probably a subreddit for it: /r/TwoXChromosomes, for example, has lots of good relevant lady content and is a great place for positive discussions and support.

➤ There's no limit to how many accounts you can make, so feel free to create a "throwaway" account if you want to ask for advice on a personal issue that you'd rather not link to your main identity.

➤ The troll is strong with this one. Not all Reddit users are knee-jerk sexist neckbeards, but there's a reason they have that reputation. It's incredibly easy to fall down a Reddit-hole of upsetting posts, so choose your subreddits carefully and stick to the ones that are positive and fun (/r/MakeupAddiction, anyone?).

➤ For added safety, take advantage of Reddit's old-school sign-up system (no logging in with Facebook here!). It's also a good idea to keep your Reddit persona unattached to your accounts in other Internet realms (that means creating a unique username, too).

## Kingdom: Forums/BBS (bulletin board systems)

**CURRENCY:** Text posts, sometimes with images

**TERRAIN:** Subforums on specific topics, populated with "threads," or individual discussions

Forums are the most classically internetty of the Internet Kingdoms. Usually organized around a very specific topic or interest—Harry/Draco slashfic, Jensen Ackles, creating authentic replica weapons for cosplay—forums are an excellent place to be...whoever you want to be. Seriously, if you want to be known only as Celstasa the Blood Elf, just throw up an avatar, and a Sin'dorei you shall be. For that reason, forums are great places for role-playing (typing out action as a particular character with another person/people in character, like telling a collaborative story), but they can also serve as tech support for games or MMOs or just a great place to swap hi-res scans of Hiddles smoldering at the camera.

> You'll need an account to post and, sometimes, even just to *read* a forum, so sorry, lurkers. Fortunately, it usually won't have to link to your true online identity, so your Inara/Mal RPs will all be safe from your Facebook friends.

> Threads in a subforum are usually displayed in descending order of most recent post, so if your question/fanart/RP request goes unanswered and slips to page two or three of results, you can "bump" it with a new post (which can literally just say "Bump!"). Don't go crazy, though—two or three bumps maximum, or you might get banned for spamming.

> Good moderators will keep a forum running smoothly, booting abusive users, deleting irrelevant or spammy posts, and mak-

ing sure all posts are on topic and in the right forum. If you ever feel harassed or unsafe, report the users to your mods, and if the mods don't act, then it may be time to find a new forum. It's never okay to feel unsafe!

⧐ Create a dedicated e-mail address to use when signing up with forums (i.e., a different address than you use for your Facebook or Twitter accounts). It'll keep all your updates in one tidy inbox, and it'll give you an extra layer of anonymity, for good measure (and good sense).

One final thing, geeky gals: *Be careful what you post anywhere.* (Not to sound like your mom or your weird aunt who posts a lot of photos of her dressed-up dog on Facebook.) Anonymous Tumblrs, pseudonymous forum posts, or throwaway Reddit accounts that aren't linked to any of your personal social media accounts are usually a safe bet, but anything you post with your real name (or even Twitter handle) is basically a horcrux: a part of you, out there in the world, for as long as the Internet shall live. Even blocking someone on Twitter isn't foolproof; if your account is public, the person you've blocked can just log out of their account and head back to your profile.

I truly know how difficult it can be to bite your tongue when a coworker says something stupid that you really want to tweet, or how hard it is not to reblog that NSFW GIFset even though your dad follows you on Tumblr. But it's super, super important that you use discretion. I am mega-opinionated about nerdy stuff, and feminism, and my love of *Pacific Rim*, but I'm also employed and followed by major media outlets. We've all seen stories of employees tweeting things that directly violate policies of the company they work for (or just embarrassingly sharing their high scores on Candy Crush Saga). Don't get dragged through the press, embarrassed in front of your fam, or fired from your gig. Be cool, and text your coworker's embarrassing speeches to your roommate, instead.

# Engage! Become an Active Member of Your Fandom

Fangirling on your own behind your computer screen is fine and dandy, but once you've seen the most popular fan blogs and fan-sites, the Tumblrs with the most followers, or the message boards where everyone seems to know one another, you're gonna want in on that excellent fandom party. But how do?

Allow me to share a little fandom secret with you: we are *all* a little socially awkward and weird, but we also all love the same stuff. This combination is perfect. No one is going to judge you for the way you are or for what you're into. Plus, joining fandoms online gives you the opportunity to e-meet geek girls all over the world. Taking the plunge is scary—but I got you.

## Make Like Link and Stay Silent...

When you first venture online, it's okay to be a bit of a lurker. Read up on the blogs, Tumblrs, and message boards you might want to become active on and learn the ropes. Figure out who the mods are, what rules to follow, and how people interact. Watch for particular conventions, terms, or bad touches associated with your fandom, and be sure to stick to those policies when you do get involved.

## ...at Least at First

Once you've learned up, the next step is as simple as starting a conversation. You know what you're talking about—you have seen every episode of *Cardcaptor Sakura*, after all—so don't hold back. If you're on Tumblr, start messaging your favorite bloggers;

on Twitter, @-reply people involved in the fandom to get conversations started. Message boards usually have threads just for newbies, so introduce yourself and then find other threads you'd like to contribute to. If you're worried about being new, say so! Everyone was new once and received help, kindness, or advice; they'll usually want to return the favor.

# Be Yourself...

Once you've started talking to people, don't be afraid to put yourself out there. Start stanning for the people and things you love. Engage in friendly debates, make dumb jokes, share particularly swoon-worthy GIFsets, and let your coordinated fangirl squees echo across the internets.

# ...or Don't

If you're starting a new role-play on a forum, setting up your first fanfic account, or queuing up a new fan Tumblr with tons of Khal Drogo GIFsets, there's no need to spill all your personal deets. Create an identity based on your fandom—your followers, RP partners, and fellow ficcers won't care if you go by "Sam," "GOTgirl," or "mother-of-dragons-696969" (not that I would ever do that?????).

# You Are So Worthy

The beauty of the Internet is that it connects fangirls to fangirls, but also to—*gasp*—the creators of the stuff we love. It's true! Your favorite author, actor, or comics artist is out there with an @ handle of her very own, and chances are she'd be happy to hear from you. If she tweets something about her new project, go ahead and hit "reply" and tell her how pumped you are to see it. If you finish the last book in a trilogy and write a long squee-laden blog post about how great it was, tag her when you post it and wait—she may say thanks, RT it to her followers, or link to it on her website. Even if your particular fave isn't a social media-ite (or doesn't use her account that much), a friendly "You're so cool and I love the stuff you make" e-mail never, ever hurts. And no reply does not mean that she hates you forever. She's just busy! Trust me, when you finally see that (1) notification from her account, you're going to feel more amazing than a million muppetarms.gif.

## Extinguish Flames, Don't Feed Them

The Internet makes jerks of us all. Don't let nasty comments— about your ship, your site, or yourself—get to you. It's just like your mom told you about bullies in first grade: they want to get a re- action (or reaction GIF) out of you. Don't let them! It's incredibly hard to be the bigger person when a cutting retort is only a few keyboard clicks away, but *resist the urge*, fangirls. Keep your online presence a positive one, and block the hell out of anyone who tries to upset you.

# All the Feels: Ten Tips for Writing Terrific Fanfiction

## 1. Know Where to Go

Most fanfic writers start out as fanfic readers, so you probably already have a good sense of where the good fics in your fandom can be found. If you're still exploring, browse Fanfiction.net or AO3.org for the book, movie, or TV show that gives you the most epic feels to get a feel (har har) for what's out there. Search Tumblr for tags about your particular ship and investigate sites like LiveJournal to see if there's an established community (and, if so, be prepared to fall down a serious rabbit hole of awesome).

## 2. Pick a Pairing

The most popular type of fanfic typically has to do with the romantic pairing of two or more characters. People *love* love, and fics that let them linger with their OTP are the quickest way to get clicks. Your pairing doesn't have to be canon or even from the same universe—how awesome would a nerdy Willow/Hermione pairing be, I'm just saying—so don't limit your imagination. Fanfic is one of those rare places where you really can let your <3 decide.

## 3. Pick a Plot

There are a lot of established tropes out there in the fanfic world, story archetypes that appear time and again and are guaranteed generators of massive feels. A story where one partner gets hurt and the other has to comfort them, an angsty story of pain or unrequited love, or an in-depth character study that explores what makes your fave do what she does—all are excellent options that let you really get into your muse's head. Other classics include re-writing a canon scene from the perspective of a non-POV character, writing a prequel about a character's parents (Marauders Era, any-one?), or creating a "new season" of a show that got the axe before its time. Remember, fanfic is all about giving the people what they want, so anything that would make you positively squee to read is something you should definitely sit down and write.

## 4. Write, Write, Write

You don't have to consider yourself a "writer" to get into fanfic. If you love your OTP fiercely and have a sudden brainwave of the two of them putting ice cream on each other's noses, that's really all you need to get started.

Being nervous is okay. But if you decide not to create some-thing because you're anxious that it won't be perfect or people might not like it, you're doing yourself a major disservice. Nothing will ever be perfect (that's what good beta readers are for; see step 5). Just throw something—anything—down on paper or on screen. Even if you hate it, you still made it, and that's the hardest part. Set yourself up with a comfortable writing space, delicious snacks (and plenty of caffeine), and an uninterrupted chunk of time. Plug in your perfect mood soundtrack (check 8tracks.com for great character-inspired fanmixes) and then *write*. If you're skittish about being seen in the act, write in the early a.m. or late at night when the normals are all asleep. And back that stuff up—to a flash drive, the cloud, or e-mail. Don't lose all your precious words!

## 5. Find a Great Beta

A "beta reader" is someone who reads through a draft of your story and gives constructive criticism (anything from "Sherlock seems a little OOC here" to "OMG ahhhhhh *dies*"). If you have an IRL friend who's a fellow fangirl, great! If not, see if one of your Internet buddies would be up for it, or use the beta-finding services on sites like Fanfiction.net. Betas are optional, of course, but they're really invaluable (especially if stuff like spelling and grammar aren't your thing). And beta-ing for someone else will let you sharpen your own writing skills.

## 6. Post Away

Most people write fanfic one chapter at a time, posting in segments whenever they get the chance to update. There's a few good reasons for this approach: it gives you a more relaxed schedule (no deadlines!), it lets you get critiques on what you write right away, and it strings your poor readers along and makes them positively desperate for the next installment [evil laugh].

Even if you find yourself with a burst of inspiration and then scribble/type out six new chapters in a single night, pace yourself and space out your updates over a few days or weeks. Also, readers are more likely to return if you keep to a consistent schedule, so if they come to expect new stuff on Sunday nights, they'll become repeat customers. On the other side, try not to go totally radio silent or your following will quickly drift elsewhere. Even if all you can manage is a quick drabble chapter, your fans will appreciate it (and be glad you aren't, like, dead).

## 7. Give and Get

Of course, the best part about fic writing is knowing that it gave someone else all the same feels that you had when writing it. But the best way to get comments is to be an active commenter yourself. When you come across a fic that you love, or one that you think could use some constructive criticism, leave a helpful, positive comment. Leave notes on stories from the "recently updated" column and you're more likely to get a quick response on yours—those authors are also up at one a.m. posting new chapters.

Be specific, too; it's always nice to quote lines that you particularly love, for example, or comment on how well the author uses sensory description. Feel free to ask questions (even if they're rhetorical ones like "HOW COULD YOU DO THIS TO MY FEELINGS NOOOO?!") The goal is to start a conversation, not just leave a quick "w2g." *Never* flame (i.e., write mean, unhelpful comments), even if you're telling the author something they've done wrong. Politely constructive comments are the only way for fic writers to learn what parts of their writing need improvement. The more you read and write, the better you're going to get. It's like a sport, but without any of the horrible physical activity!

# 8. Go All the Way

No shame, ladies. There's, uh, a *lot* of sexin' up in fanfic. Everyone is boning all the time. Right now, Harry is probably banging not only Ginny, but also Hermione, and Draco, and Snape, and sometimes even Dumbledore, and maybe all at once, just because. There's a whole subgenre of fanfic called PWP ("Porn without Plot," or "Plot? What plot?"), which exists solely to sex up the characters you love. Of course, not all fanfic includes graphic sex scenes, and none of it has to. If you want, keep it as G-rated as *The Little Mermaid*.

The fanfic community has adopted the term "porn" in a largely ironic way. NC-17 fics don't exploit or hurt any real people, either commercially or sexually. Fanfic gives us ladies the ability to write the relationships we want to read about, where our faves are suddenly all about each other, and all different types of relationships—pansexual, bisexual, asexual, all the sexuals!—get equal respect and airtime. In short, if you want to do it, *do it* (hehehe).

When you're getting down and dirty, don't be shy, but don't push yourself past your boundaries, either. Use only the vocabulary you're comfortable with, and write only the scenes that make your heart race in a good way (ain't nothin' wrong with a superhot, no-sex make-out sesh). If it helps, lock your bedroom door, put on your sexiest steampunk corset, get a little tipsy—whatever works. No judgment, remember? Write whatever pairing speaks to you (slashfic math: one hot dude = excellent, another hot dude = even more excellent, therefore hot dude one + hot dude two = exponential explosion of excellence) and let the words, ah, come. When you're done and—*ahem*—cooled off a bit, don't forget to tag your fic appropriately so that it doesn't reach the eyes of anyone who's not into it.

# 9. Feel No Shame

Obviously, you're super proud of all the awesomely awkward and adorable scenes that you're forcing your characters—and your readers—through, but there's the unfortunate reality that some people, on learning that you write fic, might look down on you. Don't buy it. Fanfiction is an old, well-respected art form. Shakespeare stole tons of plots and characters from the Roman poet Ovid. A Scottish guy named Robert Henryson read Chaucer's *Troilus and Criseyde* and wrote up his own *Testament of Cresseid* and now he's studied by English majors. The Brontë sisters created stories about the first duke of Wellington and his two sons (Real Person Fic!), one of whom they eventually turned into a superhero called the Duke of Zamorna (!). There's the zillion Sherlock "homages" that popped up in the late nineteenth century, the first modern fic published in a 1967 *Star Trek* fanzine called *Spockanalia*, and the insanely popular indie-published, fan-created Japanese manga and novels called *dōjinshi*.

Point being: fanfic is not a new thing, it's not "low," and it shouldn't be treated as less than any other form of fiction. Sure, you're writing with other people's characters. But that can be a springboard to so many good things. Fanfic writers (like the *Fifty Shades of Grey* author) have gone on to score gigundo book deals, and many published novelists have admitted to a fan-ficcer past (Meg Cabot? *Star Wars*. S. E. Hinton? *Supernatural*. Neil Gaiman? *Narnia*, *Lovecraft*, and *Sherlock*). So be proud of what you do, because writing fanfic is just, well, *writing*.

# 10. Love, Love, Love It

Just in case you're still unsure, here's all the reasons why being a fic writer is beyond amaze:

- ➤ We can practice writing fiction without the fear of censorship or harsh judgment.

- ➤ We get instant feedback on our writing from beta readers and commenters, allowing us to grow as writers.

- ➤ Fanfic forms communities based on writing and similar interests in fictional characters and introduces us to new friends all over the world.

- ➤ Fanfic lets us create empowering role models for underrepresented and marginalized folks.

- ➤ Fanfic gives us the opportunity to explore sexual identities and pairings we miss out on in mainstream media.

- ➤ Fanfic allows us to critique problematic parts of our favorite things by reimagining them in a positive and helpful manner.

- ➤ Fanfic is totally, totally bitchin'.

# A Glossary of Fancy Fanfic-Speak

Fanfic is the best. But it uses categories and terminology you may have never seen at your local bookstore. Here's a quick guide to help you search for what you want and eliminate the things you don't.

**A/N** Short for "author's note," aka your chance as the author to discuss your latest chapter (or just revel in the squees and tears of your readers).

**AU** "Alternate universe," meaning some major change to the canon has been made, with a strong impact on the characters' lives. AU fics could include a *Harry Potter* fic in which the trio are Muggles, or a Xena fic in which she's tending bar with Gabrielle at some divey place in Brooklyn.

**Crossover** A fic in which characters from two completely different universes interact. You might find Mickey Mouse on the *Enterprise*, or Sephiroth solving crimes on *Law and Order*.

**Drabble** A one-shot that is exactly 100 words long.

**Femslash** Slash, but with ladies. Sometimes "femmeslash."

**Ficlet** A one-shot slightly longer than a drabble.

**Fluff** No angst, no sadness, just light-hearted, romance-y goodness.

**Gen** Sometimes you don't want romance in your fic. Gen (or general) stories are devoid of pairings or romantic plotlines.

**Hurt-Comfort** Pretty self-explanatory: one character is hurt (emotionally or physically), the other characters offer comfort.

**Mary Sue** An original character in a fanfic; typically an idealized version of the author. Example: a super-hot elf named Sam who gets it on with everyone from *Lord of the Rings*. (It could totally happen, okay?)

**MPreg** Male pregnancy. In other words, dude characters with child.

**Non-Con** Short for "non-consensual," indicating that the fic includes sexual assault. Similarly, "dub-con" implies dubious consent.

**One-Shot** A one-chapter fic.

**Plotbunny** A fun new idea for a story that hops around in a ficcer's head, like, well, a little bunny.

**PWP** "Porn without Plot," or "Plot? What Plot?" Just all-the-time sexin'. Other names for explicitly pornographic stories are "smut" and "lemon." A "lime" is when characters graphically mess around, but there's no actual sexin'.

**Round robin** A fic whose chapters are written by several different authors in turn. (Super fun to do over e-mail!)

**RPF** "Real Person Fiction," which is exactly what you think it is: stories about real (usually famous) people.

**Slash** Created in the 1960s to describe Kirk/Spock fanfic ("slash," get it? It's a punctuation joke!), the term has since come to encompass most fanfic that involves same-sex (usually male) couples.

**Songfic** A fic in which the plot is set to the lyrics of a particular song.

**Squick** A fic with themes that might make you feel icky, usually involving sexual taboos.

**UST** "Unresolved Sexual Tension," which means that two characters will have great chemistry but won't be getting it on.

**WIP** Work in progress; i.e., a fic you haven't finished (or finished polishing) yet.

**Yaoi** Anime- or manga-based fics with a same-sex male relationship, targeted toward female consumers.

**Yuri** Anime- or manga-based fics with a same-sex female relationship.

# The Ultimate Fan Creation Inspiration Generator

Fanart, fanfiction, fan whatever is amazing for the precise reason that you can do literally anything you want with your characters and setting. The possibilities for remixes, AUs, fan comics, or filk songs is absolutely endless. And that's...a little terrifying, actually. Maybe it's your first time ever Making a Thing, or you're six chapters in and totally stuck, or you just need to figure out a fresh take on your faves.

Enter the UFCIG: mix and match feels, characters, and setting to whip together an amazing fic idea, new place to doodle your OTP, a theme for your new RP, a discussion for your YouTube channel, or maybe just a really good GIFset. Pick one thing from each column and then mix and match until you find the perfect concept for your next work. Evil twin werewolves at a formal dance? Playful Victorian-era new parents? A hurt/comfort body swap on a pirate ship? The power is yours!

| FEELS | CHARACTERS | SETTING |
|---|---|---|
| Defeated | Normals | Coffee shop |
| Overwhelmed | Hipster | Desert island |
| Crazy | Goth | High school |
| Lying | Vampires or werewolves | College |
| Terrified | Mermaids or zombies | Formal dance |
| Defiant | Gender swap | Movie marathon |
| Revenge | New parents | Detective agency |
| Hate | Criminals | Library |
| Rage | Rockstar/groupie | Convention |
| Redemption | Government rebels on the run | Banquet |
| Cowardly | Internet friends | All-night diner |
| Seriously evil | Time travelers | The wedding of an ex |
| Amnesia | Struggling artists | Comics store |
| Non-con | Pretending to be married | Emergency Room |
| Dub-con | Student/teacher | Move-in Day |
| Evil twinning | Meeting for the first time | Museum |
| Intense sexual tension | This could totally be canon | Classroom |
| Adorbs cuddling | Epic face-off | Vegas |
| Friendship | Fix the canon | The Matrix |
| Absence makes the heart grow fonder | Genre swap | The Victorian era |
| Happy endings | Backstory | The CIA |
| Joy | Accusation | Pirate ship |
| Heroic | Somebody gon' die! | Merlin's court |
| Humiliating | Body swap | BDSM dungeon |
| Intimate | Have sex with each other *or else* | A cave or desert island |
| Playful | Can now read each other's minds | Cabin in northern Canada |
| Drunk | Domestic chores | Icy, barren wasteland |

# Types of Online Trolls and How to Defeat Them

Trolls are terrible, no matter where you find them. Tolkien's trolls are super strong and yet super stupid. *Discworld* trolls are giant walking, grunting rocks. And according to D&D laws, trolls keep coming back to life if you don't finish them off with fire or acid.

But there's a whole subset of trolls that, sadly, is not fictional: the people all over the world who exist solely to spread hate, wretchedness, and gloom across the entire online universe. Internet trolls will come at geek girls with reckless abandon, knowing that we can never seek out their fleshy, human alter egos for revenge. Their attacks range from garden-variety cursing to full-on hate speech about race, gender, and sexuality. Like their relatives in games, movies, and books, Internet trolls are not homogenous. Each species has its own kind of awfulness, and knowing the type of troll you are dealing with is key when planning your counterattack. Fortunately, you've got the magical codex right at your fingertips. Here's what to look out for.

## The Warhammer Troll

Are you typing on an iPhone? One handed? In a rush? These trolls don't care. They're embarrassed by you, mortified that you would *dare* post "alot" when you really meant "a lot"; horrified that you would omit an Oxford comma; personally offended that you would accidentally use the wrong form of their/they're/there.

TYPICAL TROLOLOL: "Like I can take anything you say seriously when you put two spaces after your punctuation mark instead of one, *you dirty grammar heathen.*"

# The Mountain Troll

Screaming its valid and incredibly relevant response from so high up, the Mountain Troll speaks at LOUD VOLUMES and is incapable of disabling the caps lock key (coincidentally, all that thin air means its brain is deprived of oxygen). Troll scholars often struggle to interpret the screams of the Mountain Troll because human ears usually receive their yells as incoherent gibberish.

TYPICAL TROLOLOL: "U HAVE NO IDEA WHAT UR TALKING ABOUT LOL GET BACK 2 KITCHEN BCUZ SANDWICH"

# The River Troll

This troll takes what you say out of context, warps it from your original message, and then responds to you with a fervor typically reserved for political debates. By making everything you say horribly and personally offensive, the River Troll stabilizes its environment with a constant stream of water from its eyeballs.

TYPICAL TROLOLOL: "That one tweet where you said you prefer cats over dogs has led me to believe that you in fact want to murder every cat on the face of the planet and I am going to tell everyone on the internet everywhere what a horrible cat-killer you are!"

# The Fire Troll

Fire Trolls exist for one reason, and one reason alone: to flame you. The insults are always the same (something about how terrible you are because you are a lady), and they will never waver, no matter how much you argue.

TYPICAL TROLOLOL: "dumb betch y don't u shut ur stupid mouth stupid idiot kill urself"

# The White Knight Troll

Though you neither need nor want the White Knight Troll's help, he will ride in on his high horse to defend you from the other trolls. (Have you ever seen a troll ride a horse? It's awkward.) White Knight Trolls can sometimes morph into Nice Guy Trolls, who believe that women are just vending machines that you put Nice into until Sex falls out. They are mistaken.

TYPICAL TROLOLOL: "Guys, *leave her alone*! Ugh, I am *so sorry*. So, do you want to hang out later, or...? ...No? But I was *nice* to you! You *owe me* a date and if you *don't* you're a *bitch* and I *hate* you."

# The Olog-Hai

Tolkien trolls that can withstand sunlight and understand speech, the Olog-Hai believe that they are brighter, quicker, smarter, and better than you in literally every way. Bolstered by the magic of Google and Wikipedia, they know everything about everything, and they will argue about it until the end of time, because they are never ever wrong. Like that one guy you went to college with who still hasn't graduated after seven years but thinks he knows everything about politics because of that one Poli-Sci class he audited as a sophomore. Ergo: it is statistically impossible to win an argument with an Olog-Hai.

TYPICAL TROLOLOL: "Sure, but even Virginia Woolf said in *A Room of One's Own* that 'a woman must have money,' so *obviously* all girls are just out for cash."

# The Frost Troll

Better known as the Spoiler Troll, these creatures peruse the Internet, searching for ways to ruin your fiction-loving life. Frost Trolls subsist on the dismayed cries of disappointed fans, and they refuse to post spoiler warnings or tag their big reveals to make them easy to avoid. Particularly vulnerable to the Frost Troll are those who refuse to read the *Game of Thrones* books before the corresponding season airs, people who go on Twitter for live tweets while their favorite show is airing, and fans who DVR television and watch it after the time it airs.

TYPICAL TROLOLOL: "Wow I can't believe Rick turned every single person at the camp into zombies and then killed them with a sledgehammer on that episode of *The Walking Dead* that is literally still airing right now, that was CRAYYYZEEEEE."

# The Spirit Troll

Made of only vapors, the Spirit Troll needs to damage your self-esteem in order to survive. If you have a YouTube channel, write articles, or create fanart, the Spirit Troll will be lurking in the comment shadows, ready to elucidate on how terrible you are, remind you to stop making content, and inform you of how much it hates you. No matter how amazing or popular your content is, Spirit Trolls will always let you know that you can't please everyone.

TYPICAL TROLOLOL: "You are the worst writer I have ever read, I could have written an article better than this when I was in the 8th grade. Why don't you do us all a favor and never write anything again and I hope you die in a fiery car wreck tomorrow just because."

# Tor'Gal, the Troll Boss

Where the other trolls are relatively harmless IRL, Tor'Gal—leader of all trolls—can cause some serious damage in the real world. Tor'Gals will search out your personal, private information and post it publicly so that their troll minions can also attack you over the phone, or even in person. If you're ever confronted by a Tor'Gal, don't mess around: contact the authorities and let them know what's going on. Collect as much information on your harasser as possible (which can sometimes be tough online, I know), and make sure you catalogue, date, and screenshot every instance of harassment, especially physical threats. The U.S. Computer Emergency Readiness Team suggests starting with your local law enforcement by calling their nonemergency line and reporting online or cyber harassment; if they can't help you, go to your local FBI field office (which you can find at www.fbi.gov/contact-us/field). IC3.gov, CyberTip.ca, StopCyberBullying.org, and WiredSafety. org are also helpful.

TYPICAL TROLOLOL: "I can't believe a girl would have the audacity to try and get a game on Steam. Here's her phone number and address so you can tell her *just how much* you hate her game *in person*."

# Counterattacks

Ever heard the time-honored classic, "Don't feed the trolls?" It's stuck around for so long because it works. Every type of troll has one thing in common: its thirst is real. Trolls require a constant stream of responses to their intentionally rude or inflammatory posts; otherwise, their HP slowly drains itself, and they must leave to seek other prey. By denying them attention—their very life-blood—you disempower the trolls, leaving them to rage into the vacuum of the Internet, affecting no one.

But that isn't a great long-term solution. The major problem with the Theory of Ignore Them Until They Go Away is that it silences awesome geek ladies like ourselves. Sure, refusing to respond to the trolls ensures they'll have to run away from this battle, but it can also make you feel scared, shushed, or shamed. Even worse, the troll will probably just lumber off to its next lady-victim. Because geek girls deserve to leave their mark on the Internet— and on the occasional troll, too—here are a couple of quick and easy methods for allowing your voice to be heard across the realm.

## Counterattack 1: Lois Lane, Girl Reporter

Almost all forms of social media have a system through which you can report and block users who spew hate speech, harass others, or post violent or threatening content. Even old-school message boards have moderators that wield the Diamond-Encrusted Anti-Troll Warhammer of Permanent Banishment. If you're being trolled, report them to the proper outlets and block them from ever responding to you again. If you have supportive Internet friends (and you're a fangirl, so you probably have a bunch), get them to report and block your trollnemy too.

### Counterattack 2: Mia Fey, Ace Attorney

If you're being trolled over something you believe in, sometimes you can turn that troll into an agent of good. Instead of responding directly or privately to your troll, add a period in front of your @-reply on Twitter or post your answer publicly on your Tumblr. Now, when you drop knowledge in your response, it's not for the troll's benefit; he is merely the conduit through which you are able to educate the rest of your followers. Continue to ignore any follow-up responses from your original trolls—or any trolls who might follow in their tracks—but do so knowing that you might have influenced at least one lurker on your feed. Think of it as taking that twisted stream of troll vitriol and turning it into a rainbow that would flow freely from a unicorn.

### Counterattack 3: Jade, Proficient Photographer

As soon as things turn ugly, make like the badass protagonist of *Beyond Good and Evil* and start snapping pics. Use the screenshot function on your computer to grab as many .jpgs as you can of name-calling, hate speech, or any kind of threat whatsoever. Be sure to grab the troll's username and a timestamp, if possible. Don't assume things will stay live forever; a permalink will do you no good if the troll deletes the slimy posts. If things escalate to the point where you're feeling seriously unsafe (and want to approach law enforcement), you'll want a record of what was said and when.

### Counterattack 4: YoSafBridge, Second-Hand Man Eater

If the trolls are coming at you with horrible names, terrible language, or ridiculous arguments, first: laugh about it. Trolls can't stand positivity and shrink away from the sounds of lady-laughter, retreating slowly into the darkness of their cave dwellings. Now, instead of engaging the troll directly, simply make the original comment public: retweet, reblog, post it to your feed with all the troll's social media information attached. Not only will your followers go after the troll with the hatred of one thousand angry ninjas (or pirates, relax), you're also exposing the troll's hate speech to the world.

It's important that fangirls not suffer the wrath of the troll in silence, because silence is tacit approval. Exposing troll speech to the world reminds the public that these things are happening, rad geeky ladies are being harassed, and that's not okay. But always make sure you do whatever makes you feel safest. Your safety online is the number one priority, fangirl, so never feel bad about staying silent if you feel like that's the best bet. I do it all the time.

Now that you know how to identify, manage, and even attack the myriad of trolls you'll be exposed to, go forth and post without fear. Don't forget, we're all here to back you up…though it can't hurt to take a quiver full of Flaming Arrows +2, just in case.

# Wheaton's Law: Don't Be a Dick

Fangirls are passionate people! Emotions run high in fandom, and that's a good thing; we wouldn't love our favorite shows or celebs so much if they didn't give us crazy feels. The Internet gives us a space where we can express all of our opinions and emotions immediately, even in places where not everyone agrees with you.

But it's important to remember that we're all on the same side in fandom, though it doesn't always seem that way. Even if you don't share the exact same opinion as another person, we are all still fangirls. You wouldn't go up to someone in person and say horrible things to their face, so don't do it online, either. It can be tough to resist—anonymity makes these things easy, especially in the heat of the moment—but turning to kindness will make you feel better in the long run. Respecting other fangirls' opinions is incredibly important, even if you don't agree with them. Plus, karma's a bitch, what goes around comes around, whatever you want to call it. You want to put out positivity onto the Internet in the hopes that you'll receive it in return. And don't forget, things live online *forever*, so don't let that ugly post about how you hate someone's hair color follow you around for the rest of your life.

So even if someone likes Jake and Finn better than Fionna and Cake, remember that you're both *Adventure Time* buds. If someone doesn't think that Steve Rogers is *clearly* bisexual, you can still bond over your shared love of Captain America. Really, with any ship war, stan-off, or canon argument, keep in mind that discussions are okay, but flame wars are not.

In short, always follow Internet god and *Star Trek* alum Wil Wheaton's immortal words of advice on the topic: "Don't be a dick." Apply this rule to your whole life, including offline, and it will serve you well.

Interviews with

# Jamie Broadnax,

# Ashley Eckstein,

# Erica Schultz,

# and  Beth Revis

# JAMIE BROADNAX

◇ ◇ ◇

creator of Black Girl Nerds,
writer for MadameNoire and
Afropunk, and VP of digital for
the SheThrives Network

@JamieBroadnax

### What does the word "fangirl" mean to you?

It means someone who is a fanatic of a specific culture, hobby, or art. Fan-girls can be into cosplay, video games, computer programming, books, or science.

### How has being a geek positively influenced your life?

It's allowed me to come to terms with my identity and never apologize for who I am and what I am into. Being a geek can be daunting because some people may not understand your fandoms. However, by "owning your geek," you embrace your eccentricities and are not afraid to live outside the box. That is the beauty of being a geek.

### What advice can you give geek girls for their careers or personal lives?

Own your identity and celebrate your fandom. If you are a geek girl who is into video games, which is dominated heavily by male geek culture, be unapologetic in your passionate hobby and find other geek girls who share your fandom. True geeks focus their time, energy, and resources into their fandoms and not other people. The relationships you build with others because of your fandom will happen naturally. Home in on what you love most and find that geeky hobby that reaches into the deepest desires of your heart. Once that moment happens, you can do whatever you want to do and have tons of fun while doing it!

# ASHLEY ECKSTEIN

◇ ◇ ◇

voice actress (Ahsoka Tano in *Star Wars: The Clone Wars*, no big deal), creator of the Her Universe fashion line, and champion of fangirls everywhere

@HerUniverse

### What does the word "fangirl" mean to you?

I have always liked the name fangirl and have worn my fangirl badge with pride and honor. Most people consider it synonymous with the sci-fi and fantasy worlds, but I also think it extends to other areas of interest, like cooking or sports! As female fans, we bond over our interests. And I think it's exciting that we share our interests, even if they are different!

### How has being a geek positively influenced your life?

I have made lifelong friends just by sharing geeky interests. For so long we were bullied for having geeky interests, and now I feel like the geek community has banded together to create an embracing, supportive, and safe environment. I'm so grateful for the relationships I've made. I'm proud to be a geek!

### What advice can you give geek girls for their careers or personal lives?

Our tag line for Her Universe is "Dream Your World. Be Your World. Flaunt Your World." This is advice I try to live by. "Dream Your World" means to figure out what your dream is. "Be Your World" means to take your dream and be it, turn it into a reality. "Flaunt Your World" is the fashion/fangirl side of the advice that says it's okay to be a proud fangirl and look cute while showcasing your love!

# ERICA SCHULTZ

◇ ◇ ◇

writer and cocreator of *M3* and
writer for Marvel's *Revenge: The
Secret Origin of Emily Thorne*

@EricaSchultz42

## What does the word "fangirl" mean to you?

"Fangirl" and "fanboy" aren't terms I choose to implement, simply because virtually every time I hear them invoked, it's associated with something negative. True, I have a button on my jacket that says "Fangirl" but, as of late, calling someone a "fangirl" or "fanboy" is accompanied by eye rolls or pedantic sighs. I'm a fan of a good many things, and maybe that makes me a fangirl. Either way, just like what you want to like, and live and let live.

## How has being a geek positively influenced your life?

I was pretty much raised in the sci-fi/convention culture. Loving sci fi, fantasy, and "nerd/geek stuff" was part of my DNA. I guess the only thing it's done is taught me from an early age that it's okay to have an overactive imagination and to dream about distant stars. I've met so many amazing people through my three-plus decades and had great conversations about comics, *Star Wars* (my personal favorite), *Star Trek*, and all other types of "geek" things.

## What advice can you give geek girls for their careers or personal lives?

Don't listen to haters. There will always be someone, somewhere, who has something negative to say. Don't listen to that person. Be strong and confident in who you are and what you enjoy. As long as you're not a serial killer.

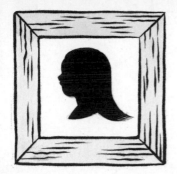

# BETH REVIS

◇ ◇ ◇

*New York Times* best-selling author of the Shades of Earth trilogy and proud Whovian Browncoat

@BethRevis

### What does the word "fangirl" mean to you?

It's pure, unbridled enthusiasm for something. A fangirl has no shame: she loves what she loves and she doesn't apologize for it, she doesn't restrain herself, she's not meek. Girls are often told to be quiet little ladies. A fangirl doesn't care about being quiet. She does exactly what she wants, courageously, to celebrate the things she loves.

### How has being a geek positively influenced your life?

When I was younger, I was very much concerned about fitting in with the "it crowd." I was never a popular girl, and I hung out at all the periphery edges of the circles. When I entered college, I was pretty alone. None of my friends were at that college. The university was so large that there really wasn't an "it crowd." There were just people doing the things they wanted to do. It was a very freeing experience. I realized that it didn't matter what people thought of me—I was happy being a geek and working with other geeks. I found true friends in my shared passions, and I learned that real happiness comes from that deep, honest place within myself that geekdom allowed me to embrace.

### What advice can you give geek girls for their careers or personal lives?

Don't ask for permission to be who you want to be.

# chapter three

# Geronimo! How to Survive Conventions

Fangirling on the Internet is fantastic, but what about IRL? Conventions are the best place to meet new friends, awesome creators, and even your fave celebrities. There's panels to see and costumes to wear and oodles of exclusive swag to snap up— all of which you're going to want to do as soon as possible. So study up and your next con will rock your world, blow your mind, and change your life (srsly).

# Adventure Time! Conventions Are Awesome and You Should Go to There

The Internet! It's so rad! It's over 9000 in excellence level for geek girl culture! You've got fandom-specific communities; you can interact one-on-one with celebs and creators; you can buy unique, hand-made merch; you can admire talented cosplayers; and you can even make a bunch of new fangirl friends (or fan girlfriends?) who you already know share at least one of your very specific interests (like Faunlock fanfic). But what if there was a place almost exactly like the Internet…except in real life?

*There is.* It's called a *convention*, and it's geek girl heaven, where dreams come true, and the land of misfit toys *all in one*. Conventions are where everyone in the nerd world comes together: fans, actors, writers, artists, cosplayers, shops…you name it, a con's got it. Held in convention centers or hotels, cons traditionally run over a weekend (which, in con terms, can often mean Thursday through Sunday). Admission options range from basic one-day pass to full VIP weekend package, with prices scaling accordingly. Whether you head to the huge, general-interest expos, like San Diego Comic-Con, or more specific gatherings, like BlizzCon or IndieCade, you'll be surrounded by like-minded people who would never even *think* about judging you for your imported Hatsune Miku action figure collection or your printouts comparing Jared Padalecki to various moose.

All cons have a few key elements in common. First, there's the con floor. This is the big, open space that gets filled with various nerdalicious booths and tables. The "Vendor" or "Exhibitor" side of the con floor is where you'll find the big-name peeps you recognize—DC, Marvel, Ubisoft, Nintendo, etc. The bigger the con, the bigger-name corps you'll see setting up life-size Pikachu playgrounds for you to climb all over. You'll also find smaller sellers here—local comic book stores, retro game dealers, and those guys with the anime mousepads where the girl's boobs are the wrist rest (surprisingly comfortable, FYI).

Second up is a subsection of the con floor (and my personal favorite portion of any convention): Artist Alley. Imagine if every crafter, stitcher, webcomic creator, and fan artist you have ever loved on Tumblr, Etsy, and DeviantArt conveniently settled down into several aisles, selling their sweet swag to you, in person. *That's* Artist Alley. Creators flock to conventions from far and wide because they know you want to meet them (even if you embarrass yourself while telling them how amazing you think their NC-17 fanart for *The Wolf Among Us* is).

As if that wasn't enough, the third feature of most cons is the celeb encounter spaces: panels, signings, and photo ops. Good cons will attract a solid roster of comic, gaming, sci-fi, and anime guests that you can catch in a few different ways. Included in the cost of admission are panels, which are basically big auditorium sessions where the celeb guest gets up on stage (either alone, with other cast members, or with a moderator), you sit in the audience, and they just *chat* to you for an hour or so. (You can even ask them questions! It's lovely.) For a small fee (okay, sometimes a big fee—*Matt Smith and Karen Gillan group shot*, I'm looking at you), you can also hit up your idols for an autograph or a photo op in smaller locations on or around the con floor.

I hit my first con when I was eighteen—my mom and I flew to Vancouver, British Columbia, for a fan-run *Stargate* convention called Gatecon—and this con (and the many cons I later attended with my mom, because geekiness is genetic) taught me a few things. First, I learned that a great majority of con-going sci-fi fans were—*huge gasp*—ladies! (It seems like the ratio at Stargate conventions is one dude for every thirty women, and even big cons like Emerald City have a higher number of female attendees than male.) Second, I realized that interacting with all the members of the GateWorld forums—from the fifty-year-old Kiwi grandmother to the super-rad French trans woman—was way more excellent in real life than it was online. Suddenly we had photos together and stories to share and we were actual friends, with faces and geeky tattoos and great hair.

Conventions can seem intimidating if you've never been to one (or even if you have!). Hitting up a con means you'll be surrounded by masses of people, overwhelmed with things to do and see, terrified of meeting celebrities, and anxious about all the lines. But I'm here to tell you that the pros way outweigh the cons when it comes to…cons. (Sorry.) It's worth ten times the insanity that awaits you on the convention grounds for all the lovely memories, purchases, and connections you'll make over the weekend.

So if you're a con virgin, let me help prep you for your first experience. And if you've been to so many cons you've lost count, there's sure to be a few tips and tricks in the pages ahead that will help you get everything out of your future cons (and let's meet up at the next one, because we should be besties). No matter what, remember to have fun. And make sure you're wearing comfortable shoes. (No, but seriously.)

# Fantastic Cons and Where to Find Them

Conventions range from general interest to super specific, so investigate within your fave fandoms to see if there's a smaller con just for your people—221B Con in Atlanta, for example, caters just to Sherlock Holmes fans (of every adaptation, too, so don't go hating on *Elementary*).

If it's a bigger con, you can usually expect to pay anywhere from $20 to $75 for single-day tickets (the most expensive day is typically Saturday), $100 to $300 for weekend passes, and up to $500 (or more) for special VIP packages. Here are some of the biggest, best, or just all-around awesomest cons.

## Anime!

### Anime Expo—Los Angeles, July 4 long weekend
www.anime-expo.org

What better way to celebrate America's birthday than to indulge in some excellent Japanese culture? Anime Expo—AX for short—is the largest anime and manga convention in North America. It takes over the LA Convention Center every July 4 weekend, filling it with the most *kawaii* goodies, exclusive panels, and larger-than-life cosplay you can imagine. Plus, tons of English dub voice actors live in LA, and the AX team is great at pulling in talent from overseas, so AX always seems to get out the best stars for you to see.

SECRET BONUS: AX is a 24-hour con! All-night events include dances, tabletop gaming, and (of course!) karaoke.

## Otakon—Baltimore, early August
www.otakon.com

This three-day festival in Baltimore celebrates Otaku culture in the best way, including anime, manga, movies, singers, and all kinds of other excellent pop culture. The staff is made up entirely of volunteers (which means everyone is a fan!), and the Baltimore Convention Center is massive—Otakon has one of the best Dealers' Rooms of any con in the country. (They're starting a second, smaller Otakon in Las Vegas soon to test out some new ideas, so keep your big anime eyes open for that, too.)

SECRET BONUS: Otakon takes over an entire HD theater for the length of the con to screen an almost constant stream of animated movies. If you're more the party type, you can't miss the Otaku-rave, where amazing Baltimore-area DJs spin for the cosplaying crowds.

## Anime North—Toronto, end of May
www.animenorth.com

Canada's biggest anime con is spread over six hotels in the north end of Toronto, and the cosplay is crazy. *Everyone rocks cosplay* and because the con is so spread out, most cosplayers just wander around in the city all day. It's an amazing sight to behold. Totally fan run, AN has raised over $80,000 for children's hospitals through events like their Charity Auctions.

SECRET BONUS: Tons of the voice cast of the original *Sailor Moon* dub live in Toronto full-time, so if you've ever wanted to hang out with Serena and Darien, AN is your best bet.

# Gaming!

**Penny Arcade Expo: PAX Prime** (Seattle, end of August), **PAX East** (Boston, mid-April), **PAX South** (San Antonio, end of January), **PAX Aus** (Melbourne, end of October), **and PAX Dev** (Seattle, end of August).
*www.paxsite.com*

The folks behind the *Penny Arcade* webcomic created these all-gaming cons, which have exploded into the annual must-attend events of the games world. If you show up to one of their five different cons, you can expect to play all the next big games way in advance, watch some crazy tournaments, and meet fellow hard-core gamer fans. PAX has also banned booth babes (yay!) and added a "Diversity Lounge," which is an encouraging step in a great direction.

**SECRET BONUS:** Kristin Lindsay, Penny Arcade Project Manager, says her favorite part of PAX is "the quiet spaces; table-top free-play areas, the handheld lounges, and the rooms where people are doing demos" because these areas are places where she (and you!) can learn new games and meet new friends. It's the most personal level of PAX!

## California Extreme—Santa Clara, mid-July
*www.caextreme.org*

And now for something a little different. A "Classic Arcade Games Show," California Extreme is the oldest of old-school gaming cons—a massive collection of coin-operated pinball machines and game cabinets. Play the original *Donkey Kong* as it was meant to be played—standing and sweating—and watch in awe as the pros attempt world records.

**SECRET BONUS:** Leave your giant bag of quarters at home because every machine at California Extreme is set to free!

## Gen Con—Indianapolis, early August
www.gencon.com

This convention has been running in Indiana since 1968 (!), making it the longest-running gaming convention in the world. They've even trademarked the phrase "The Best Four Days in Gaming." Given Gen Con's old-school roots, you might not be surprised to learn that the convention is big on tabletop gaming, but they've got goodies for PC gamers, too.

**SECRET BONUS:** The Game Library and Pick-Up Play Area are amazing for making new gamer friends. Bring your own game or rent one from their extensive collection, grab a table with some other con goers, and get your tabletop on.

---

**Pro Tip:** Cons like the Electronic Entertainment Expo (E3), Game Dev Con (GDC), and the Consumer Electronics Show (CES) are huge, but you can attend only if you have an industry or press pass. Sorry, fangirls. Fortunately, most of these events are live-streamed online, so it's easy to participate from home!

---

# Creating!

## IndieCade—Los Angeles, early October
www.indiecade.com

This Culver City con is a little different from your typical fan con. Over the course of the weekend, you can take part in educational seminars, participate in game jams, and design your very own indie game. Known as "the Sundance of gaming," IndieCade started off as part of E3 but spun off when it got super popular. Now, indie developers from all over the world come to showcase their amazing work.

SECRET BONUS: Like a poetry slam, the IndieCade GameSlam lets game devs get up and quickly showcase their games in ninety seconds. You're going to meet so many good games in so little time!

## Maker Faire—everywhere, all the time
www.makerfaire.com

Created by Maker Media (the folks behind *Make* magazine), these conventions celebrate innovation and creativity and welcome creators of any kind. Techies, crafters, teachers, students, engineers, authors, artists, vendors—all are welcome to show off their amazing inventions. There are Maker Faires throughout the world, from New York City to the White House to Trondheim in the U.K., with mini Maker Faires from Montreal to Oslo.

SECRET BONUS: The Faires have something for literally everyone, but favorite past panels include "The World Record Paper Airplane" and "Robotic Fashion and Intimate Interfaces." Attractions have included life-size mousetraps and the "Game of Drones."

## South by Southwest—Austin, mid-March
www.sxsw.com

"But, Sam, isn't that a music thing?" you ask. Yes, SXSW does feature a music and film festival, but it also has a great interactive media component. Featuring the newest (and often wackiest) tech innovations (like foldable motorized scooters and phone-based Breathalyzers), SXSW draws celebs and entrepreneurs to shill their good shtuff.

**SECRET BONUS:** In 2014, Shaq showed up to announce *Shaq-Fu 2: A Legend Reborn*, and then played as himself in the original *Shaq-Fu* (one of the worst games of all time). That's the kind of awesome weirdness you can expect at SXSW.

# Books & Indie Comics!

## GeekyCon—various locations, end of July (usually)
www.geekycon.com

The ultimate summer gathering for book nerds! Since its first con in 2009, GeekyCon programming has expanded to include panels with YA authors, wizard rock concerts, book signings, and a Lit track with workshops and networking for aspiring writers. Though this con was founded by a Harry Potter fansite, it's become a must for all kinds of readers. The location changes yearly, but past host cities include Orlando, Chicago, and London, England.

**SECRET BONUS:** Far from a boring keynote speech, the opening ceremony is a "fully fledged geeky musical" featuring "as many special guests as we can wrangle onto one stage." (!!!) Previous celeb performers have included Amber Benson (of *Buffy* fame) and members of Internet sensation Team StarKid.

## Toronto Comics Arts Festival—Toronto, May
www.torontocomics.com

For the more serious indie comics fan, TCAF is a low-key (no cosplay here!) weekend festival that features tons of comics-related events. Held in a huge public library in downtown Toronto (and totally free), comics creators from around the world can exhibit their wares (think cool mini comics and zines), and readers can attend panel discussions, gallery shows, and programming for kids.

SECRET BONUS: Local gaming collectives team up with TCAF to concurrently put on Comics vs Games! a mini con that includes panels with illustrators, comic creators, and game makers on the differences and similarities between the comics and gaming industries. (Also check out the Bit Bazaar, where artisans sell their gaming-related goodies.)

## YALLfest—Charleston, early November
www.yallfest.org

This Charleston, South Carolina, festival is devoted to—you could even say *obsessed with*—young adult literature. YALLfest usually draws over fifty big-name authors (past guests include Sarah J. Maas, Stephanie Perkins, Kami Garcia, Scott Westerfield, and Gayle Forman) for panels, discussions, and signings. The best part? All the programming is *free free free*!

SECRET BONUS: Okay, I lied. The best part is definitely the famous YA Smackdown, where every author guest at the con has to get up on stage, form teams, and compete in storytelling games for the Golden Pie award. It's basically an awesome author rap battle.

# All Things Geeky!

## San Diego Comic-Con—San Diego, late July
www.comic-con.org

SDCC is the mothership of all cons. It's enormous. It has the best stars. All the biggest companies come out. Huge announcements are made. Entire casts show up to panels. Oh, and the crowds are the biggest. But don't be put off by the three days you'll have to spend in line to get into the big panels in Hall H. SDCC has some of the best smaller panels and an amazing con floor. So many big-name brands and networks that you don't find anywhere else (like BBC America) have booths, and it's so profitable for artists to table that you'll definitely be purchasing some greatness.

SECRET BONUS: *The swag.* SDCC is such a big deal that companies give tons of stuff away for free. (If you catch one of the big panels, you'll probably even get a "swag room" pass—your one-way ticket to a room of free stuff. *Nerd nirvana.*)

## New York Comic Con—New York City, early October
www.newyorkcomiccon.com

It's the SDCC of the east! Big, loud, and fun. You get all the enjoyment of San Diego Comic Con *and* you get to be in New York City. Bonus! It's run by pro-con team ReedPOP (who also work with PAX and C2E2), which means it's incredibly well organized and never feels quite as insane as SDCC, even though attendance is similar. The cosplay is great, the panels are a blast, and at night you can head over to Broadway for a show. What's not to like?

SECRET BONUS: New York Super Week runs the week leading up to NYCC and continues during the convention. It takes all the goodness of the con and spreads it out over a full seven days all across NYC, including events like nostalgia nights, trivia contests, podcast tapings, and nerd improv shows.

## WonderCon—Anaheim, mid-April
www.comic-con.org/wca

WonderCon gives you that crazy con feel but without the crushing terror of trillions of fans. Also it often gets some great advance film screenings for test audiences; past previews have included *Watchmen*, *Kick-Ass*, and *Batman Begins*. Plus, there's always a great selection of vendors selling back issues of comics. WonderCon's proximity to Los Angeles means that all the big stars still come out (even though it's not as big a deal as SDCC). That means you're much more likely to be able to see your faves without having to stand in line for days!

SECRET BONUS: The WonderCon Children's Film Festival—free with your badge—features the best short kid-friendly films from the Los Angeles, San Diego, and San Francisco International Children's Film Festivals. Great if you have a little fangirl in tow!

## Emerald City Comic Con—Seattle, end of March
www.emeraldcitycomiccon.com

This three-day Seattle convention has all your great comics, gaming, and television goodness—but, more important, it's known for being incredibly good to its attendees. ECCC is run by fans, advocates an amazing "Cosplay Is not Consent" policy, and has earned a stellar rep as a creator fave thanks to the fantastic comics and fan community in Seattle.

SECRET BONUS: Even if you can't make ECCC, the convention live-streams all panels on flipon.tv. That helps mitigate the con envy.

## Dragon Con—Atlanta, first weekend in September
www.dragoncon.org

Spread out over five hotels in downtown Atlanta, Dragon Con has a little bit (okay, a *big* bit) of something for everyone. With around fifty thousand (!) attendees, it's definitely a larger-scale con that focuses on sci-fi and fantasy and includes programming on things like short films and YA literature. Music is also a big draw, and tons of great bands like GWAR and Spock's Beard have played the event. Everyone I've ever known who has been to Dragon Con comes back saying it's unequivocally their favorite.

SECRET BONUS: Don't miss the annual Dragon Con parade! Thousands of guests, cosplayers, societies, and more register to participate, and the result is epic. It's basically like if you took the inside of a con and paraded it down the streets of Atlanta. Nuts.

## GeekGirlCon—Seattle, mid-October
www.geekgirlcon.com

This awesome Seattle con is a celebration of ladies from every facet of geekery. It started at SDCC in 2010 as a panel called "Geek Girls Exist," and from there a group of volunteers got together online to form the first GeekGirlCon the very next year. The convention is still entirely fan run, so not only can you attend, you can also apply to help organize it! GGC has a great set of values that welcome everyone, encourage community, and make the event super fun.

SECRET BONUS: If academia is your jam, GGC has tons of amazing lectures focusing on critically dissecting and unpacking your fave mainstream nerdy media. Want to have an in-depth discussion on the representation of gender in video games? It's going to go down here.

# Do, See, and Get It All at Your Next Con—No TARDIS Necessary

So, you did it. You bit the Bullet Bill and you bought tickets for a con. Congratulations! I'm so excited for you! But...now what? Here's a timeline breakdown of what to prep and when.

## Stardate: A Long, Long Time Ago

The con is months, or even a full year, away. You feel like you have tons of time. But don't trust your feels in this case, ladies—these things tend to sneak up on you like little hobbitses. And you don't want to forget something vital; after all, you'd much rather be Tony Stark *with* the Iron Man suit than without it, right?

### Teaming Up

Don't wait until the day before the con to determine which scoundrels are going to make up your con team. If it's a big expo, chances are you're going to have to buy your tickets way in advance (up to a year), so make sure you have a solid group together before making your purchase. Group con-going has tons of benefits: it can help lower hotel and gas fare, and cosplaying as a themed group is, in my opinion, the most fun you can ever have dressing up at a con. Members of your con-clave can save seats for one another at panels, reserve spots in lines, or grab swag for events you can't attend. Plus, the con experience is always more fun when you have someone to share it with, before, during, and after.

But I'm not going to tell you everything is awesome-force-powers and leave out the awkward you-might-become-super-evil side effects. Traveling with a group means you're always going to be worried about someone—hoping everyone is having fun, keeping track of your friends and their schedules, wondering how mad they'll be that you got a con-exclusive Rocket Raccoon plushie and they didn't—and you may have to make some concessions on what you might get to do or see en masse. Also, finding seats together in busy panels is hard. If you have three or more geeks on your squad, you might have to sit closer to the back or split up.

## Flying (Han) Solo

On the other hand, if you're by yourself, you can do *whatever you want*. You don't have to argue, coordinate, or talk to anyone all day if you don't want to. Panels are incredibly easy to attend because there's always a few single empty seats between groups of people right at the front of the auditorium. And while you're in line or sitting on your own, you are surrounded at all times by *new* friends. (The people next to you in the "How to Draw for Marvel" panel? Amazing artists. The couple in front of you in line for the Tom Welling autograph session? *Smallville* nerds with a mind-blowing theory you've never even considered. Get these people on your Tumblr dash, stat!) If the con is in your hometown, you can make IRL friends for life. If not, you'll get some amazing new Internet besties. It might seem daunting and scary and awkward and all those things we try really hard to avoid in everyday life, but the truth is, literally no one but you cares, and once you get there you are going to have the best time. Just walk in pretending you're Batwoman in her civvies, which always works for me (and gives you a great don't-mess-with-me face as an added bonus).

Of course, it's important to always be safe when attending a con alone, so make sure to stay in contact with friends and family on the outside during the day and keep your phone charged up!

## Bounty Hunting for Tickets

Plan your strategy well in advance, especially if you're heading somewhere like SDCC, NYCC, MCM, or FanExpo Canada. Find out if you need to do anything before tickets go on sale, like registering for an account. When you know the date and time that tickets are going live online, be ready. Make sure you sign on *before* the sale time, then keep refreshing until the tickets pop up, and don't leave the virtual waiting room once you're in it. (You can always try opening the website on another device for a second shot at the virtual queue, or have several friends on different computers.) Con ticket-buying can be stressful, agonizing, confusing, and sweaty—but stick it out. Once you've hit "Accept" on the credit card payment page, you are going to be so, so stoked.

## Seek Shelter

The logistics of finding a place to stay can be complicated and pricey. For instance, San Diego Comic-Con runs hotel lotteries to determine where you can stay. But at many smaller cons, you can grab a room in the same hotel as the event. You can also look into independent sites like AirBnB or Couchsurfing to score a place to sleep that's nearby and (hopefully) cheap.

## Getting to a Galaxy Far, Far Away

Book your flights and hotel well in advance. If you need a passport, make sure yours is up to date. It never hurts to type up a little travel itinerary so that you've got all your confirmations on hand when you get there. If you're carpooling, figure out how you're splitting gas way ahead of time (trust, it avoids many potential future arguments), and while you're at it, check the con website for parking info. If you're staying at a hotel, some cons offer a free shuttle service to and from your accommodations, though those can be *really hard* to grab at the end of a con day, when every other convention-goer is also trying to get back to the hotel via shuttle.

Alternatively, look into public transportation. You'll be able to get a real feel for what it's like to live in the con city, and it will probably be way cheaper than grabbing a cab or paying for parking. But double check for delays or closures the morning of the convention. Once at a con in the dead of winter, I cosplayed as a battle-worn Rule 63 Booker from *BioShock Infinite*, but I forgot that the subway was closed that day, and I left my wallet at home (a total n00b mistake), so I couldn't grab a cab. Lesson being: check your public transit in advance, ladies. Don't let this be you.

## Plan to Shoot First...

Cons usually release the daily schedule a few weeks before the event, so print one out and spend some quality bonding time together. The con floor is always a good time—there's so much to see and buy, you could easily spend all weekend just roaming the aisles. But if you stick to the floor, you'll miss what is truly the greatest part of the con: panels, photos, autographs! Cons typically run only two to four days, so organizers have a ton of content to squeeze into a short amount of time, which, sadly, means that a lot of the things you might want to do will probably overlap.

First, pick the panels and celebrity sessions you absolutely must attend. Don't forget, even if nothing is technically at the same time, you need to factor in anywhere from thirty minutes to hours of time spent standing in line for the event. If none of them conflict, *yer a wizard, Harry*, because that is magical and impossible. Sessions will likely overlap, and if the con is big, you'll need to add in the time it takes to navigate a packed convention hall to get from one room to the next. Also find out if they empty the room between panels—if they don't, you might have to grab a seat in the room at 8 a.m. just to catch the panel you want to see at 4 p.m.

## ...or Second

Once you've got your schedule down, pick a couple back-up options. Just because a panel is smaller, or something you might not necessarily love in advance, doesn't mean it won't be awesome. Some of your best experiences will be at smaller, unexpectedly excellent panels, I promise. I once hit a panel for *Continuum* before I'd ever seen a single episode, and that one con hour convinced me to start watching the show the very next day. (Another time, before a *Grand Theft Auto V* panel, I ended up watching a promo panel for a movie that is actually called *Big Ass Spider!* So...that happened.)

Most important, try not to overbook. You're going to want moments of freedom to do things like eat, hit the restroom, and shop the con floor. If you get too attached to your plans, you're going to miss out on a lot of the essential con experience. And if you're traveling a long way, don't forget to plan at least one thing outside the con. Explore the city you're in, make reservations at restaurants not in your hotel, wander the downtown. Sure, you'll be tired. But you're in a new city, and you can catch up on all that sleep once you're home.

## Identify Yourself

I cannot stress enough: *don't forget to print your tickets at home.* You'll exchange these at the con for a lanyard, badge, or wristband that'll let you in. If the entrance booths open early, trade in your printed tickets for a badge or wristband ahead of time so you don't eat up hours of your first day waiting at the con.

If you have time, go online and print some social-media calling cards before you go. You'll be meeting so many new people you'll want to stay in touch with—be they artists, celebs, Internet friends, line buddies, or new seatmates—but painstakingly explaining where all the dashes go in your Tumblr username is time consuming and awful (and sometimes cons are so crowded that the Internet shuts down entirely). Solution? Calling cards! Think business cards, but for friendships. Include all your Internet handles—Twitter, Facebook, Tumblr, fanfiction site, wherever you can be found—and if you're an artist, include some of your work. You can even add a snap-and-scan QR code if you're feeling snazzy.

# Stardate: T-Minus 7

You've done all your long-term planning, and the con is only a few days away. If you're journeying to lands far and wide, you're going to need to start that horrible, dreaded thing we all try to avoid as much as possible: packing.

## Blast Off

Whether you're going the distance or sticking close to home, try not to overpack. You're going to be doing a lot of purchasing at the convention, so start saving money far in advance, pack only the things you absolutely need, and fold up a big empty tote or duffel bag on the bottom of your suitcase. That way, you can fill it up with all your con goodies.

And do try to remember not to go crazy on the con floor. Yeah, that Pop! Vinyl figure is super cute, but you can also find it at your local comic book store. Try to load up on Artist Alley or con-exclusive finds that you can't grab anywhere else.

## Suit Up

I know I said this before, but *comfortable shoes*. They are literally all that matters at a convention. I know you want to look super hot because we all want to impress our faves, but just trust me on this: heels, unsupportive flats, or anything else generally uncomfortable is not worth the pain. Convention centers or hotels usually have concrete floors, and those kill not only your feet but your *entire body* if you're not rocking responsible kicks. If you absolutely must wear flats, use gel inserts for cushiony support. If heels are the only choice for your cosplay, break them in ahead of time. Otherwise, stick with something cute and casual like Chucks or Vans. Your back will thank you on Con Day Three.

Outfit-wise, this is your one chance to wear something totally geeky or obscure and have people readily compliment you on it, so you might as well go all out. Jeans and a nerdy tee are classic, but you should also consider your Dalek dress or Deathly Hallows leggings to really let your stylish geek girl out. Pack a sweater or jacket to throw on top—cons are always mega air-conditioned, and you don't want to spend the day freezing. If it's a summer con with outdoor lines, don't forget sunscreen and sunglasses. No premature wrinkles for these nerd-girls, thank you very much.

Also, don't forget to pack all your con essentials in your bag (see page 129).

## Jack In

Most cons have official social media accounts on Facebook and Twitter (at the very least), and you should definitely make a point of following their feeds during the con. (I know I was just talking about how cons are great because they're *not* the Internet, but I'm not telling you to go completely offline for the weekend. Is that even possible? Do people even do that? How?? Why????) Keep tabs on the con folks for tweets about line lengths, guest locations, scavenger hunts, giveaways, etc., and also follow whichever celebrities and friends you're most excited about meeting that weekend. Comic artists, for example, often run contests through their social media for free sketches. Lastly, if you're traveling in a pack, use your powers of social media to triangulate your con-gang's location.

# Stardate: LIFTOFF

All your planning is done. Your bag is packed. You've got your pass. You've finished marathoning *Orphan Black*. It's con time. But if you think you're ready to head inside just because you've done all this planning, you know *nothing*, Jon Snow. There is a lot to deal with once you're through the front doors.

## Halp, What Is Things

It's here. Finally. The thing. You're arriving and it's glorious and *holy balls is that the line of people waiting to get inside*?! Yes, cons are crowded. When you first get to the con location, you might find yourself a bit taken aback by the sheer volume of people you see waiting to get in. But it's okay! If you've brought things to keep you occupied (see page 130), you're good. Everyone *will* get into the convention, including you. Try not to stress about it. Take some photos of cosplayers as they arrive (or be photographed if you're in costume), get excited, and double-check your plan of attack for when you cross the threshold. That way, you'll be first in line for con exclusives or a sweet, sweet autograph from your fave.

## What Even Are Words??

If you're lucky enough to get a seat at your dream panel, don't be too shy to get up and ask a question; the guests do this all the time, and they're used to it. A good panel question is something everyone in the audience will understand and enjoy. Do a little research so you're not repeating questions the star has already answered a thousand times. Silly in-universe questions ("Which of your characters would make the best personal chef?" and the like) always go over well and get good laughs. Just take a few deep breaths before you approach the mic and try to keep your voice steady. You'll do great.

## Photo How Do??

The picture from your photo session will likely be rushed (and you'll probably be nervous-sweating), so definitely prepare what you want to say. This isn't the moment to give the guest a big speech about how much you love them—you just paid a bunch of money for their photo, so they know. Walk in, say *hi* and *nice to meet you*, and then quickly request whatever pose you're going for. But think of a fun pose or action before you head in to your photo op; you've maybe got a grand total of ten seconds with the celeb once you're in front of the photo wall. Browse other photo ops with that particular actor available online; some people (like the *Being Human* cast or John Barrowman) are known for being up for anything, whereas other stars (like adorable Stan Lee) might be a little more reserved. For better or worse, the more hilarious the photo, the more likely it is to make its way around the Internet.

Also, make sure you're good with your outfit; for example, if you don't want to be immortalized as an Ent in your Billy Boyd photo, you may want to consider cosplaying Treebeard on a different day.

## Then Who Was Name??

Autograph sessions are much more convo-friendly than photo ops if you want quality time with your star of choice. Depending on how many people are in line, your autograph moment can last anywhere from thirty seconds to five minutes. This is when you get to shake their hand and tell them how much you love their work, or share a story about how one of their performances changed your life, or show off your epic tattoo of their face, if that's your thing.

Here's a weird secret: if the star is particularly well known in the nerd world for one thing, try to compliment his or her work in something obscure instead. Like, sure, you loved Tom Felton as Draco Malfoy, but if you tell him how much his performance in *Belle* impressed you, I guarantee you'll see his face light up and get some new stories out of him. You might even extend your time at the autograph table.

Last thing: don't forget that a lot of stars have rules regarding photography during autograph sessions. If it's strictly forbidden, don't try to sneak in a photo or ask for one once you're talking. Just be chill and follow the rules.

# Stardate: Post-Mission

So that was the best weekend ever, right? Aren't you glad you went? You found some great new geeky collectibles, met so many new friends, got a photograph with your fandom babies, had people compliment your cosplay, and were on a high for, like, four straight days. But highs like that are inevitably followed by a crash, and the post-con blues are no joke. It's hard to get back into the reality of daily life after you've basically spent most of the previous week in nerdy nirvana, but there are some things you can do to ease the after-con pain.

## 28 Days Later

After the weekend you'll probably get hit with something called "con crud." Cough, exhaustion, sore throat, whatever—con crud covers all the disgusting bases. Though there's no single cure, getting as much sleep as possible post-con is key—if you can take the Monday off school or work, do it. Then load up on orange juice for vitamin C, eat as healthfully as possible, and have a couple introvert-friendly nights on the couch. This would be a great moment to marathon a new show.

## First (and Second) Contact

Post-con fizzle can also hit you emotionally. If you're feeling lonely, go through the cards and papers you collected at the con, add your new buds on social media, and start reminiscing. Post and tag all your photos right away, so you (and everyone you know) can immediately relive the awesomeness. Try on new clothes you got, frame your new art, take your figures out of their boxes (maybe). Now's the perfect time to circle back to the friends you made waiting in line for that panel!

## Dollar, Dollar Bill, Y'all

Cons are like black holes for your wallet, what with collectibles and Artist Alley and *I must have a photograph with Matt Smith here have every money I have*. If you overshot your budget, don't fret—you'll do better next time. Besides, studies have shown that spending money on experiences ultimately makes you much happier than frittering it away on random stuff (though those Sailor Moon plushies won't hurt, either).

## Costume Drama

You spent long hours (and probably a lot of money) making the Aayla Secura costume of your dreams, you strutted your stuff around the con floor, and now you've got beautiful memories (and smokin' hot photos) to prove it. But it's not exactly the kind of outfit you're going to wear on the street. Hanging on to your cosplay duds is always an option—stuff like boots and leather pants can be upcycled into your next creation—so if you have the closet space, go ahead and set aside a dedicated storage area for your con outfits. Be sure to get proper hangers, garment bags, and wig cases to keep everything in tip-top shape; store leftover makeup in a cool, dry place. If you'd rather try to recoup some of your investment, you can also sell your secondhand costume online (see "Resources," page 197).

## Rinse and Repeat

The best, final means to banning the post-con blues? Start planning for the next one. Obviously.

# [MAIN MENU] [SAVE] [LOAD] [MAP] [JOURNAL] [X INVENTORY:]

**Bag:** Bring a reliable and roomy carryall that isn't going to kill your back or shoulders; a cute backpack or cross-body messenger bag works great. If you're cosplaying, hang with a friend who's willing to do the schlepping for you, sew pockets into your costume, or create an in-costume tote that works (like the Ramona Flowers circle purse!).

**Water:** Stay hydrated! You'll be on the go all day and you're going to get parched. Purchasing water at a con is unreasonably pricey, so bring your own. Also, you're much better off with water than coffee or soda, which will in fact dehydrate you.

**Cash:** Most vendors and artists at a con don't take debit or credit, so purchases tend to be cash only. Sure, cons have ATMs, but the lines typically stretch all the way back to Narnia. Just hit a bank machine on your way in.

**Chargers:** Whatever devices you have on you are going to drain, and fast. Empty hallways or restrooms are usually a good bet for outlets, and if you have room in your bag and want to be a con hero, bring a power strip so everyone can recharge their gadgets at the same time. It's also worth investing in a battery-powered charger for times when you can't find an outlet.

**Camera:** I get by with my smartphone camera, but if you've got a great digital, you might as well use it to get solid close-ups of all the goodness. Be aware, though, that some cons (like Wizard

World) have restrictions on DSLRs, cameras with removable lenses, and professional videography equipment, so check the policy beforehand.

**Gum or mints:** Don't meet Nathan Fillion with bad breath.

**Sharpies:** Make every chance encounter an autograph opportunity.

**Lip balm and moisturizer:** In addition to being cold, cons are always dry.

**Hand sanitizer:** There are like a million germy people at this con, and you really don't want to get sick.

**Watch:** Your phone battery drains fast if you're using it to check the time every four seconds. Get old-school and rock a rad timepiece.

**Empty poster tube:** Your new prints, posters, and photos are far too valuable to get bent out of shape. Bring an old wrapping paper tube or poster tube to roll your goodies into for safe-keeping.

**Comics bags and boards:** If you're a comics collector, you're going to need a few empties to throw your purchases into.

**Business or social media calling cards:** To keep in touch with everyone you meet at the con. Hand these out prodigiously!

**Something to do:** You'll need to pass time in line (save your phone battery for other things). Books—if they're not too heavy—and e-readers are always a yes, as is a portable gaming system (DS, Vita, whatever). If you're feeling friendly, bring a small card game to play with the people around you.

**Aspirin:** Like I said, long day, big crowds. Better safe than sorry.

**Food:** Convention center food is never healthy and always expensive. To maximize your energy, fill up in the morning with a big protein-y breakfast, grab something at the con for lunch, and eat a good dinner. You're going to be super hungry during the day, what with all the running around and the line standing, so bring snacks like fruit or energy bars.

**Patience:** In excess.

# All-Nighter Booster Pack:

If you're at a gigantic con like SDCC and you're dead-set on getting into the biggest panel of the year, you might find yourself in the epic-est of all epic lines: the overnighter. (Remember the SDCC 2012 when devoted Browncoats got in line for Hall H three days in advance to catch the Firefly Tenth Anniversary Panel? Of course, Joss Whedon *himself* eventually walked the line and took pictures with everyone in it, but still.) This sort of fandom takes a special, expert-mode level of planning, so in this case, you'll want to add the following items to your inventory:

**Extra food and water:** 'Cause, obviously.

**A pillow:** Necessity. Any pillowcase is fine, and don't let anyone tell you otherwise, anime body-pillow fans.

**Eye mask and earplugs:** For when you need peace and quiet.

**A jacket:** It might get chilly!

**Toothbrush and hairbrush:** Stay human.

**Makeup bag:** No eyeliner can survive multiple nights, no matter what the commercials will have you believe.

## Cosplay Emergency Booster Pack:

If you can also solicit a nice non-cosplaying friend to carry a bag of essentials for you, here are the must-have just-in-case tools to head off a wardrobe malfunction.

- Flat shoes, for when your poor feet have inevitably had enough
- Ibuprofen and gel insoles, for the same reason as above
- Safety pins
- Fabric glue
- Wig cap, bobby pins, and hairspray
- Clear nail polish, for nylon runs
- Eyelash glue and extra lashes
- Contact lens solution and case
- Double-sided dress tape
- Matte face powder/blotting paper
- Extra lipstick/eye makeup/body paint/etc., for touchups
- Stain stick (like a Tide To-Go pen)
- Antistatic spray

# OMGYES; and, How about No? Things You Should Definitely Always Do (and Not Do) at Cons

## 👍 Affirmative:

**Do have your camera or phone out:** You never know when you'll spot a celeb on the floor or when your OTP will spontaneously start kissing during a panel. Don't miss memorializing the moment because you weren't photo ready!

**Do ask for contact cards:** If you pick up something rad in Artist Alley, grab the vendor's card and put their work on social media. You want to give them love for the great stuff they make, right? Same goes for the new friends you've met in line or at panels. Solidify your new friendships by sending them a tweet or a Tumblr ask after the con.

**Do be all over social media:** If something amazing happens at the con, share it on your accounts for the world to see. People who can't be there (your fangirl buds, your Internet friends, me) have to live vicariously through someone, so it might as well be you!

**Do seat hop:** Most cons don't empty rooms between panels. If you're sitting way at the back for the first panel of the day, slowly make your way forward as the room empties slightly between each panel. By the time you get to the panel you really want to see, you could be sitting right up front!

**Do be responsible when saving seats:** If you're hitting the con with a giant gang, don't stand in line by yourself and then try to save an entire row for your crew. Not only is it rude, it's also incredibly difficult. People will fight you for those seats. Limit yourself to saving a maximum of two seats; if you need more, bring another friend to save another two.

**Do set a budget:** Trust me when I tell you you're going to want to buy all the things, and your wallet is unprepared. Hit an ATM precon, take out only as much cash as you're willing to spend, and when it's gone, it's gone. Remember to ration it wisely!

**Do buy quick:** Exclusives and particularly fantastic artist originals sell out *fast*, so if there's something you've got your heart set on, it's best to grab it right away. Same goes for personalized sketches: if you want an artist to draw you something, hit them up first thing in the morning the first day you're there. Their sketch schedule is going to fill up fast, so you want to be early in line. And make sure you have a design idea in mind before you ask. If there's anything you're not quite sure you want, leave it to the last day and see if you can pick it up at a discount.

**Do cosplay on the right day:** If you're cosplaying only one or two days of the convention (and a couple of days in normal-person clothes can be nice), make sure you save it for busy days. What's the point in putting tons of effort into your outfit if no one sees it? By wearing your costume when the con is packed, you'll get a million people wanting to take your photo, which way increases your chances of becoming Internet cosplay famous. *The dream.*

**Do venture to the rim:** The lure of the big-name booths at the center of the con floor is unavoidable (Nintendo! Marvel! Disney! So much goodness!), but chances are they'll be crammed, and you probably already know what they're offering. For surprisingly excellent discoveries, head to the outside of the con floor; the tables and booths along the edge of the room, hidden in the corners, or out in the corridors have lots of great stuff, too. You might find excellent book publishers with geeky books (*ahem*), clubs you can join, like the *Star Wars* 501st or the *Firefly* Browncoats, or indie webcomic artists whose work you'll love.

**Do manage your expectations:** I know I said this already, but try to attend expecting to just go with the flow and enjoy moments as they come. That way, when amazing things happen, you'll be delighted. And if you miss out on something, you won't be facing crushing disappointment.

**Do be nice and have fun:** All weekend. Standing around in lines for ages, crushing crowds, sore feet, getting hangry…all these things can make you cranky and generally not fun to be around. But we're all in this together, so try to stay kind, especially to con volunteers. They're there to help, and a smile and some understanding will go a long way. Though it can be easy to forget amid all the chaos, you're at the con to have a good time. A *great* time. So whenever you catch yourself freaking out, take a couple deep breaths and remind yourself that this is *superhappyfuntimes*.

# 👎 Negatory:

**Don't expect to sleep much during the con.** It blows, and by the last day you're going to be mad exhausted, but that's the price of packing all your fun into one fantastic weekend. You're up early to get in line; you're staying out late to hit all the parties. Five or six hours of sleep a night might be all you get, so make sure they're good.

**Don't harass anyone, ever.** Sounds obvi, sure, but things like glomping, attack hugs, or even taking cosplayer photos without permission counts as harassment. Also, if a cosplayer is sitting or eating, that's not a great time to ask for a photo. Just be super respectful, to everybody, always.

**Don't wait until the last day to buy something you have your heart set on.** Yes, lots of vendors and artists discount things on the final afternoon, but if you're looking for one thing in particular, you run the risk that it sold out ages ago. Use the discount day to pick up things you might not have considered at full price and be pleasantly surprised with your finds. (Example: the small stuffed alpacas called *arpakasso* I randomly picked up at the tail end of a con, aka the best purchase I've ever made.)

**Don't cut in line.** People will get *so mad*. You are not prepared for this level of anger.

**Don't go up to the mic at a panel and ask the celebrity, "Can I get a hug?"** Everyone at a con hates the people who do this.

**Don't bring gifts for the guests.** They usually aren't able to accept. (Would *you* take a cookie from a stranger?) A kind word or a thank-you will do just as well.

**Don't be afraid to ask!** If you're in line for an autograph and there aren't any posted rules about photography, it never hurts to ask the handler if you can grab a quick photo. If you see a celeb out and about, and you're super polite about it, you can ask for an autograph. If you don't know how to find a room or a panel, ask a volunteer. Approaching new people is scary, but it's totally worth it.

# The Cosplay Prime Directive: How to Rock a Costume

Cosplay! I know what you're thinking. It's that thing where pro-costumers and artists make huge costumes, wear them to cons, and then get famous on TV, right? Wrong. I say thee nay, fangirls!

Cosplay is short for "costume play," and it's something anyone can do. (Yes, lady, even you!) All you have to do is find a character you want to be and then make it happen, no expertise required (though you can totally go all-out if you feel like it). Creating a costume yourself is incredibly rewarding, whether you're grabbing items from thrift stores, sewing pieces from scratch, or going hardcore to craft them with molds and worbla. But if you're not feelin' that, you can also commission a costume from an experienced cosplay crafter or find something online and modify it to fit your needs. When it comes to the con, attending in costume is fantastic because you can either really become that character all day (if acting is your thing) or just be super rad and take pictures with a bunch of people who love you and your outfit. If you get your cosplay game together in advance and plan a group cosplay—all your friends as the Sailor Senshi, say?—then I guarantee your con experience will be the absolute most fun.

If you've never tried cosplay, you might feel embarrassed, nervous, or even frightened. That's understandable! Every new thing worth doing is a little scary at first. Here's the thing: Your costume does not have to be perfect (no one's is, not even professional cosplayers'). You don't have to look exactly like the original character. And you don't have to talk to anyone you don't want to—ever. Cosplay is just about becoming a character you love for a day, trying on a different persona, and showing off all your hard work. Try it and you'll be glad you got past your nerves, because cosplaying at a convention is *the most fun ever*.

Before venturing into the cosplaying crowds, you might want to give a quick read-through of these "The Articles of the Cosplay Federation" (or, if you will, the Cosplay Prime Directive).

## 1. Consider your con scene.

Think about where you're going. If it's Anime Expo, it's probably best to stick with an animated character. PAX? Make it gaming related. BlizzCon? You better be rockin' the *WoW*. At big cons like SDCC or Wizard World, you can pretty much take the "if it fits, I sits" approach and cosplay as whatever the hell you want.

## 2. Cosplay a character you love.

*Anyone* can cosplay as *anything*. Ever! There are no rules about ethnicity, gender, size, whatever. Be a Sailor Scout of color, dress up as the Doctor and bring a dude who will play your Amy Pond, rock a corset and a blaster and go as Steampunk Lady Han Solo—and don't ever let anyone give you flack for it. There's no point in spending your time and energy on a costume you don't care about, or putting together a "unique" getup just for the sake of wanting to cosplay.

For my first cosplay, I approached it Spock-style: I had a purple wig, so I googled "characters with purple hair," but none were really from my fandoms, and I wasn't jazzed about the outfits, either. Ultimately, I ended up scrapping the purple hair idea in favor of making my own TARDIS dress, which was *way better*. I got to express my Whovian feels to everyone in the most public way possible. Invest in your costume as an excuse to share your fangirling with the world at large.

# 3. Do your research.

Find detailed photos of the character and really examine them with a critical eye. Is that outfit something you're going to be able to pull off at your skill level of costume creation? Will you have to spend a bunch of time learning how to sew or fabricate? Do you have that time?

If the outfit seems too difficult to re-create, you have a few options. Consider wearing a character's alternate, less-common outfit; for example, if you really want to be FemShep from *Mass Effect* but can't build a full suit of armor, stick to her nice N7 civvies dress. Or wear a few key accessories that suggest your character's overall vibe (goggles, gloves, a red-and-black Harley Quinn-esque T-shirt). You can also find a talented artist to commission a custom outfit, but make sure that she is experienced with similar styles *and* has the time to finish your cosplay before the convention. Also, although there are many bargains to be had online, be wary of overseas discount vendors; if something looks too good or cheap to be true, it probably is. Artists with a good rep will get you your money's worth, so read reviews and pick one with quality cred.

# 4. Start early.

Make a list of all the items you'll need for your finished cosplay and where to find them; local craft, sewing, or hobby stores are always a good start, but don't overlook thrift stores and charity shops for cheapie basics. If you know how to sew, you don't even need to draft your own designs; basic Butterick or McCall skirt or dress patterns make great customizable bases. And since your purse is unlikely to match your cosplay, make sure your outfit has pockets or compartments in which you can store your essentials.

# 5. Keep it safe.

Most cons prohibit any kind of sharp metal or real weaponry. Make sure that your sword or bow and arrow are made of harmless foam, and that the red safety cap is still visible on your blaster. Etsy and eBay are great resources for props or accessories you can't fabricate yourself, as are local costume (or even toy) shops. If your costume requires recoloring any part of yourself—body paint, colored contacts, eyelash glue, etc.—make sure you test those products out before the day of to determine sensitivity or allergy issues.

# 6. Think ahead.

How are you getting to and from the con while in costume? Will you need to bring pieces to assemble or put on at the show? If you'll be spending a lot of time indoors, make sure your outfit is comfortable to wear all day in an air-conditioned building. If you're going to be frequently outside in sunlight, try to stick to something lightweight, with waterproof makeup. And one last thing, which no one ever tells you, but seriously: *figure out how you're going to pee in it*. You will be totally miserable if you can't get out your relevant bits to do your business, so put your outfit together in detachable pieces whenever possible.

# 7. Know your time limit in costume.

If the outfit is large, heavy, or bulky, it's okay to cosplay for only a half day. Head back to your hotel to change at lunch; or, if your con has a coat check, stash your civvies there. Your safety, health, and happiness always come first. (Unless the fate of the world and/or galaxy hangs in the balance, in which case we can talk.)

# 8. Socialize!

Once you're at the con, fully decked out, you should expect to have the craziest day of your life. Depending on the size of the con you're attending, you'll get photo requests anywhere from every ten minutes to every ten seconds. Either way, definitely plan your entire day around your cosplay. *Everyone* is going to want to admire and pose with you, so it's going to be hard to get anywhere without having to stop every five steps (which is flattering and fun 90 percent of the time, but *terrible* when all you want to do is get to the bathroom or go back to your hotel). If you're worried about how you'll look in photos, get all Tyra and practice in the privacy of your own home. Remember the look and strike that pose every time someone asks you for a shot.

# 9. Never feel bad for saying no.

You are mistress of your own domain, and you're allowed to refuse any photo request you so desire. If someone makes you uncomfortable, or if you just damn well don't feel like posing, you can say "Not now, thanks" without having to give a reason or offer an apology. If you're getting a sketchy vibe, ask the photographer or videographer where your image will wind up on the Internet. If they're for "personal use only" or you're not down with the photog's press outlet, you don't have to consent. Same goes for touching: if you're okay with people throwing an arm around your shoulders, that's awesome; but if you'd rather fans stay an arm's length away and give you a solid fist-bump instead, that's awesome, too. If you're usually timid, rehearse your sweet cosplay poses and your stern-but-polite refusals in the bathroom mirror beforehand. Think of them like acting lines—you *are* in character, after all. Just be that bad-ass lady or dude on the inside, too, and you'll be just fine.

## 10. Stick up for yourself.

Here's the most important thing of all: cosplay is not consent. Just because you're wearing a costume doesn't mean anyone has the right to your image, to touch you, or to say inappropriate things to you. If you're ever harassed by anyone while in costume (or not in costume, for that matter), *report them immediately*. Make notes on your cell phone about what happened, report it to a security officer or con volunteer, and tell everyone you know in the cosplay community about the offending creep. Any reputable con worth giving your time and money to will have a policy in place for situations just like this. If they don't, don't attend it.

## 11. Enjoy every last amazing minute.

Cosplaying is the *most* fun you can have at a convention. So many people are going to compliment your hard work, want to know more about your character, and might even follow your adventures in cosplay for years to come. Enjoy it to the max and really get into wearing someone else's skin for a while (in the least squicky way possible). This is a rare opportunity to really become your fave, so have a blast! And feel free to blast anyone who tries to stop you.

# Gather Your Party and Venture Forth? Meeting Friends, Celebs, and Dates IRL

Here's the thing: I'm, like, *way* suave on the Internet. When no one has to see my face, and I can type and retype sentences as many times as I want, and I can punctuate all my relevant points with cat GIFs, I'm a brilliant conversationalist.

But things are not quite so simple when you have to interact with people sans Internet. What are you supposed to do at a con, when you're suddenly faced with the possibility of meeting Internet friends, new friends, celebs, and even potential dates for the first time?

Asking people things (especially about themselves) is a guaranteed amazing conversation-starting trick (feel free to give me credit when it changes your entire social life). Your friends will instantly love you because you're interested in them, and you'll get to leave the day feeling like you are the Most Interesting Girl in the World—and you are! After all, the best way to be interest*ing* is to be interest*ed*. Beyond that, here are a few more tips for getting to know your fellow con-goers.

## Internet Friends!

There's really no better place to meet your Internet friends IRL than at a con, especially if you've got a worldwide online network of besties. We geeky gals travel from far and wide to attend cons so it's a great way to know you're all going to be in the same spot simultaneously. Plus, it provides a safe, populated, security-guarded environment for meeting Internet strangers. Bonus!

If you grab tickets to a con, make sure to post on social media that you'll be there. Once you know who among your netz friendz is going, exchange photographs via private message so that you know what the other person looks like (they probably don't look like their Natalie Dormer avatar). If they give you their number for finding-each-other-in-a-crowd purposes, that's cool; but don't feel obligated to send yours back if you're not comfortable. Suggest a recognizable location for a meetup that's well trafficked (for safety purposes) but also quiet enough that you'll be able to spot each other. If you're super nervous, bring a friend to the meetup. It's also okay to plan a few things to say to your Internet buddy—we all get tongue-tied! Even if they're not exactly as you imagined they'd be from the Internet, that's totally okay—you might not match their mental picture, either. But now that they're a real person, you can get to know this version, too.

# New Friends!

Conventions are a prime opportunity to expand your geeky social circle. Even if the con is out of town, you'll be able to continue your friendships online for years to come. And it's super easy to make new friends at a con, even if you're nervous and a little socially awkward—*everyone else around you is as well* (remember?). Wherever you end up, and whomever you sit next to, you'll have at least one major shared interest: whatever panel or artist or celeb you're waiting to see.

Start with a simple question about their fave pairing, the first episode they ever saw, or what they're most looking forward to in the reboot, then chime in with your own opinions (remembering to disagree *respectfully* if their OTP is your NOTP). If you don't quite hit it off, don't worry—it's a big con, there will be other people to talk to, and they will probably get swept up in something else soon enough. But if you do, and you spot them later on the con floor, you've already got something to talk about! Boom.

# Maybe Future Dating Friends!

Geek Speed Dating events have lately become a thing at conventions. Whether you're after dudes or ladies, the odds are always in your favor: women tend to be in short supply, so walk-ins are usually welcome. It's often arranged by category—comics, sci-fi, anime—so you'll have something in common with everyone in the dating pool. There's no pressure to approach anyone—you can just stay seated and assess your potential partners as they come round. Dispel any feelings of "What am I even doing here oh god I should probably leave this is so awkward" by reminding yourself that everybody in that room would be mad lucky to date you. Because it's true. Be kind, ask a lot of questions (always), and be the superhero of that room. The great thing is, if you like someone, you can write down his or her name; if you hate everyone, you never have to see any of them again. It's the perfect dating scenario.

# Celebrity Friends!

Potentially the most terrifying thing about a con weekend is also the most exciting: that moment when you finally, *finally* get to meet the celeb love of your life. There are a few ways to prevent total meltdown in front of your fave. First, remember that they're just a person. It's easy to build these people up because they've had such an impact on your life, but they're also just normal folks, and they don't love to be gawked at like zoo animals.

Second, keep in mind that you'll have about ten seconds at a photo op and thirty seconds (maybe more) at an autograph session, so it never hurts to plan what you want to say. If possible, try to hold off on the tears and the shaking (inevitable) until after your interaction. Trick your brain into thinking you're just talking to a friend, and things will go much better. And lastly, if you do say something dumb, remember: as valuable as you are as a fan, you're just one in a sea of faces. Chances are, they'll remember your beautiful smile, or the kind compliment you offered, and not how sweaty your hands were. Mischief managed.

Interviews with

# Laura Vandervoort,

# Kate Beaton,

# Stephanie Leonidas,

# and Lorraine Cink

# LAURA VANDERVOORT

◇ ◇ ◇

kick-ass actress and sci-fi gal extraordinaire; star of *V*, *Smallville*,
and Syfy's *Bitten*

@vandiekins22

### What does the word "fangirl" mean to you?

It means a girl who is strong, imaginative, and fun. A girl who knows exactly
what she likes and wants and can use her imagination to disappear into a
world of endless possibilities.

### How has being a geek positively influenced your life?

Outside of the industry and the incredibly wonderful fan base, being a geek
has opened a new world to me. A world of incredible characters and powerful women. It has encouraged me to pursue the genre in film and TV, always
playing females that challenge me physically, intellectually, and emotionally.

### What advice can you give geek girls for their careers or personal lives?

Simple. Never apologize for who you are. Pursue your interests...let them
flourish. Be as crazy, unique, and confident as you are.

# KATE BEATON

creator of the "Hark! A Vagrant" webcomic, and the *New York Times* best-selling comic collection of the same name

@beatonna

## What does the word "fangirl" mean to you?

I really think it's sweet. There's a sense of ownership and pride over claiming that something has meaning to you when you hear people declare it in that way. And when you're a creator and people say it to you, it's a high compliment; you make things so that they can belong to people, and here is someone saying, "I found it."

## How has being a geek positively influenced your life?

I don't know! I think it's cool that people are identifying with being geeks and nerds in a way they haven't before, because those are awesome things to be. For me, I never really put a name on it, it was just, "these are the things I like," and that was that. But, you know, identify with it or don't, it's all good! Like what you like. I wouldn't be doing what I do if I hadn't always zeroed in so hard on the art and reading that interested me, which I think is what a geek is, someone who cares with all their heart about a few things that they've always loved. To practice the thing you love is even better.

## What advice can you give geek girls for their careers or personal lives?

It's pretty simple advice, actually: just keep doing what you're doing. And your voice, your thoughts, your input is unique. If you're making things, it's that unique individuality that will help you stand out, so find it. It's probably great. If you're involved in the culture in other ways, a fan or a critic or a cosplayer or anyone at all, remember that all these things exist together, and you always matter.

# STEPHANIE LEONIDAS

◇ ◇ ◇

actress known for starring in such awesome geeky stuff as Neil Gaiman's *MirrorMask* and Syfy's *Defiance*

@StephLeonidas

## What does the word "fangirl" mean to you?

For me it's about passion. Being so dedicated to a show or character. The comic cons really opened my eyes to this; it's exciting seeing large amounts of people taking over cities for the weekends of the conventions. The atmosphere is incredible; everyone has such love and support for each other as well as for the shows, comics, and people they are there to see.

## How has being involved in the geek world positively influenced your life?

The support I've received since doing *MirrorMask* and then *Defiance* has been overwhelming. I feel so lucky to be part of that world. I've been fortunate enough to meet some incredibly talented people and amazing work that I might otherwise have never come across.

## What advice can you give geek girls for their careers or personal lives?

Be yourself and never apologize for who you are or the things you are passionate about.

# LORRAINE CINK

◇ ◇ ◇

actress, comedian, writer, and
host of Marvel's *The Watcher*

@lorrainecink

### What does the word "fangirl" mean to you?

Fangirls are female-identified humans (as well as other humanoid species and possibly androids) who claim fervent passion for a universe—real or fictional. Addendum: fangirls use a lot of exclamation points!!!! BECAUSE OMG! DID YOU SEE?!?!?!?!?!

### How has being a geek positively influenced your life?

From the time I was too little to remember, I was plunked in front of sci-fi movies and carted off to the occasional comic book convention. When I got close to age eleven I was diagnosed with a genetic hip defect—my mutant gene. But I had Wolverine. Wolverine had been filled with metal. He survived. He thrived. And for the months of walkers and rehab that followed, I could explain to other kids that I was like Wolverine. I could associate my ailment with being special/gifted/super instead of less-than. I am lucky as an adult to be able to walk without any sign of this past malady, but I will always carry that experience with me. Being a geek has given me untold strength (superstrength even).

### What advice can you give geek girls for their careers or personal lives?

Whatever you want to do—start now. No one needs to give you permission. No one needs to invite you to the table. Just do what you love. Eventually someone will see what you are doing and invite you to that table, or better yet, you'll build your own damn table. And be nice to people. Not just because that receptionist will someday be a billionaire-playboy-philanthropist who could give you an amazing job, but because life is hard and everyone deserves a fair shake. Kindness feels good to give and it's totally free.

SELECT CHARACTER

# chapter four

# Aim to Misbehave: Geek Girl Feminism

Being a lady these days is awesomer than it has ever been before. Plus, more women are becoming forces to be reckoned with in the geeky industries we love, which is why it's so, so important to be supportive of other women. Page through this chapter, support all the ladies, and come sit by us, girlfriend.

# Why Call Yourself a Feminist, Tho? Because Reasons!

## Because you think all humans should be treated the same!

Do you want every human everywhere—regardless of gender, race, class, sexuality, or fandom—to have the same rights? Then congrats: you are a feminist. Huzzah!

## Because history!

Ladies who came before worked hard to get us awesome things like the right to vote, and have jobs, and own property, and not be property! Honor those amazing women and their sacrifices with your feminism.

## Because comic books and video games aren't just for boys!

Anybody can like anything. Fact. Feminism fights for this idea.

## Because you wanna do whatever you wanna do!

No matter what you like to do, say, wear, play, read, or cosplay, you should be able to do it without persecution. Feminism is on your side.

## Because not everyone is as lucky as you!

Feminism fights for the rights of ladies and girls all over the globe to go to school, work, drive, choose whom to marry, and do many other things you might take for granted. High five.

## Because you love yourself!

Being a feminist means that you want the very best for yourself. And that's a good thing, fangirl. You deserve it!

# The Geek Girl's Litany for Feminism

I am a geek girl and I am a feminist. ◇ I embrace the word "fangirl" with open arms. ◇ I don't have to prove my nerd cred to anyone, ever. ◇ Whether I'm a comics n00b, or a fic writer typing up her next chapter, or a hard-core gamer who sometimes forgets to sleep (not that I ever do that), no one else gets to decide whether I do or do not belong. ◇ From SuperWhoLock to Shakarian, I accept all fandoms and ships as equally meaningful and important in our geek girl lives. ◇ Even if your OTP is my NOTP, I will still like you (though I may have to unfollow your blog). ◇ I can wear makeup and R2D2 mini dresses, or a Chewie T-shirt and ripped jeans, and the world has to deal with it; because a geek feminist looks however she wants and doesn't apologize. ◇ I will support empowering, lady-created media and amazing female characters who make me feel like I could be Batgirl, if I just had some yellow Doc Martens and a vigilante complex. ◇ I'm the Doctor, not a companion; Buffy, not Bella; nobody's sidekick, love interest, or token female. ◇ I'm driving this ship. ◇ I'm a fangirl, a feminist, and a force to be reckoned with.

# A Glossary of Secret Feminist Code Words, Lingo, and Slang

Check your privilege! Don't mansplain to me, bro! Ugh, patriarchy! Feminist media uses a lot of words that are complicated and unfamiliar and make it sound like there's a giant top-secret feminist Illuminati Reptilian New World Order brewing somewhere behind closed doors. (Which there totally isn't!) (*Or is there?!*) (Mua ha ha!) In all seriousness, here's a primer of your basic feminist terms, decoded and made easy.

**Agency** The ability to act for yourself, aka a thing you definitely want. If someone is trying to control you, or speaking for you, or not letting you make your own decisions, they're denying you agency.

**Derailing** Entering into a discussion on feminism only to change the topic so drastically that you can't even continue the original discussion. Like when people start calling out your grammatical errors instead of commenting on your thoughts—this train's off the rails!

**Feminism** The belief that people of all genders deserve equal rights, everywhere. *Boom.*

**Gender** How you identify, you human being, you: Male! Female! Both! Neither! Many feminists believe that gender is a social construct that has nothing to do with your physical anatomy. If your gender and your sex match, then you're *cisgender*. If they're opposites, you may consider yourself *transgender*. Other people may identify as *bigendered*, *genderqueer*, or with neither or both genders.

**Gender binary** The dichotomy that splits everything (even stuff that has no basis in sex or gender) into "male" and "female." (Video games are for boys! Skirts and dresses are for girls!) The gender binary is a social construct (i.e., made up by people, as opposed to biologically determined). Ever had to explain to a disappointed little girl that she can't get a Batman toy with her Happy Meal because that's the "boy" toy? Yeah, ick. Gender binary at work.

**Intersectionality** Intersectional feminism takes into account anything and everything that can marginalize people: gender, but also race, sexual orientation, ethnicity, physical ability, and class (for example, that being a woman of color means you could be subject to both misogyny and racism). Thinking intersectionally is important because identities are complex, and there's no such thing as a default human.

**Male Gaze** Film critic Laura Mulvey coined this term to describe when the audience is put in the position of the (heterosexual) male perspective: sexualized female characters, close-up booty shots, everything framed as if it were coming from a dude brain. In a lot of media (think stupidly sexy beer ads), the male gaze is the default.

**Mansplaining** When a guy explains something to you, usually because he assumes that he, as a dude, knows more about it. Occurs when a guy tells you period cramps really aren't so bad, or that female superhero costumes *need* boob windows because they're *empowering*.

**Misogyny** Fearing or hating women. Someone who engages in this is called a misogynist (although "jerkface" is acceptable under your breath).

**Objectification** When you take away everything about a person that makes them a person (e.g., agency, personality, favorite flavor of ice cream, etc.) and see them as just an object for sexin'.

**Othering** The idea that, with any two groups, one is "us" (the default) and one is "them" (i.e., other). In nerd-world, othering can often manifest as the "*we're* geeks and *you're* girls" division, which doesn't check out. There's no such thing as a default human!

**Patriarchy** A gender-based hierarchy wherein men and masculine traits get all the power and respect, and so-called female things are seen as weak and of lesser value. Patriarchal thinking is bad for *everybody* because it imposes impossible ideals on humans of every gender. Dudes are expected to be beefy, aggressive alpha males. Ladies gotta be sexy, silent, and submissive. Thanks for nothin', patriarchy.

**Privilege** All the things about you that might make your life a little easier than the lives of other people not in your (usually majority) group. When someone tells you to "check your privilege," they're reminding you to recognize where you're coming from. For example, if you're straight and white, your experience differs from that of queer girls of color. And that's okay! Privilege-checking simply asks that you acknowledge your personal biases and listen to perspectives from all different kinds of people. No prob.

**Sex** Determined by your biological bits (read: hormones and your p and/or v). Sex isn't always a one-or-the-other thing, either; you can be intersex or otherwise nonbinary.

**Sexism (or gender discrimination)** Prejudice or mistreatment because of sex or gender.

# Nope: Five Myths about Feminism in Need of Busting

Surprising no one, there are a lot of misconceptions floating around the Internet about what it means to be the geeky, empowered gals that we are. If we were to believe them all, we'd probably be under the impression that a fangirl feminist is a cross between an imaginary unicorn, a giant bra-less ogre-lady, and a super-sexy succubus who goes around cutting the dangly bits off every man she meets. (Which, okay, sounds kind of amazing, and I think I would like to read a comic book about that.) Obviously, that's not the case, so I'm here to clear up a few things that you might have seen floating around the great intarwebs.

## Myth 1: Men can't be feminists.

*Au* so *contraire*, nerdettes. To take just one example: Sir Patrick Stewart (aka Captain Picard, double aka Professor X, triple aka best friend of Sir Ian McKellen) is both a huge self-proclaimed feminist *and* a huge amazingly awesome proponent of ending violence against women. Dudes who believe in the equality of the sexes, or the crappiness of the patriarchy, or the idea that women are better for more than just staring at creepily—*all* are welcome under the feminist banner. So if you've got a male friend who wants onboard, let him in the club! (And definitely imagine the rest of this section being read to you in Sir Patrick's dulcet tones and dashing accent. Engage!)

Some guys might wonder why the movement isn't called "equalism," if it's about equality. A fair question! Thing is, women are generally marginalized compared to men, so naming the movement "feminism" helps keep women's rights a priority.

# Myth 2: Any girl with nerdy interests must be faking it for male attention.

Have you ever gone to a convention or a tabletop night and had someone quiz you on your nerd cred? Probably yes. If you believe the Dorito-dust-encrusted denizens of Internet trolldom, the Fake Geek Girl is a woman who feigns interest in classically nerdy hobbies like video-gaming or comics-reading. Fake Geek Girl accusations can be blatant or may come out in millions of different little petty actions or comments called microaggressions ("I bet you've never even read a Superman comic") that can make you feel abnormal or unwelcome in the nerd community.

But here's the thing: geekdom is undergoing a massive cultural shift. You know as well as I do that the *Revenge of the Nerds* stereotypes of the '80s no longer apply. As more ladies take ownership of the nerdy content they love, we are the community, just as much as anyone else. Plus, there's no "right" way to like something; if things like sci fi or video games or comics didn't appeal in more than one way to more than one kind of person, they would never be commercially successful—so find appeal in them in whatever way you want. You are a real geek if you feel it in your feels. After all, as nerd-girl band the Doubleclicks say, "There are no fake geeks, only real jerks."

# Myth 3: Feminist geeks hate men.

Feminist geeks don't hate men! Not by a long shot. I mean, we've got some pretty amazing examples: Captain America, Batman, any stand-up citizen guy (with or without a cape) is A-OK by us. (We just wish that, for every comic, movie, or TV show about a superhero, we could get one about a superheroine as well.) Feminism is all about equality. The idea that we hate men and want to take over the world is a bummer stereotype perpetuated by the media, and it harms our awesome fight for the future of humanity. Feminism is a movement for anyone and everyone, and—I'll say it again—being a feminist does not mean that you don't like dudes. It just means that Wonder Woman and Black Panther deserve their own movies as much as Superman does, and that when they finally hit the big screen, we're gonna be all *shut up and take my money* about it.

## Myth 4: Cosplayer = booth babe. And both are fair game for grabbin'.

Cosplayers are women who spend months, sometimes years, perfecting their convention costumes as an expression of their love for a specific character or franchise. We cosplay because we love one particular character, we're great at sewing, or we work out twice a day and feel fantastic when we dress up as Psylocke. Or because we've never worked out a day in our lives and neither has Ramona Flowers and *it doesn't matter* because Ramona is a bad-ass and dressing up like her makes us feel bad-ass, too.

We *don't* cosplay because we want strangers to grab (or even stare at) our butts or boobs.

Booth babes are *not* cosplayers. These women—aka promotional models—are paid by companies to stand by a stall at a convention, sometimes while wearing a costume, and drive attention to a particular product. Booth babes belong to an agency. They're models for hire. This is their job. Their costume is not something they made themselves (or even got to choose).

So what do cosplayers and promo models have in common? No one gets to touch them unless they say it's okay. No matter how revealing the outfit, consent is *required*.

# Myth 5: It's hypocritical to criticize sexy lady superheroes, because dude superheroes are also sexy.

Ever heard of false equivalence? That's when you set up an apparent logical correlation between two things where in fact none exists. A prime example is the whole "Sure, lady superheroes are super sexy, but guy superheroes are super muscley! They're both objectified and unobtainable, and they present unfair body stereotypes!" Here's why: in comics, overly sexualized female characters and testosterone-tastic male characters are both *male fantasies*. The women are male sexual fantasies; the men are male power fantasies. Have you ever looked at a vein-popping, neck-bulging, Liefeldian drawing of Captain America and been like, "Mm, yeah, I super want to cozy up with *that* guy"? Probably not. Because that image is for *men* to look at and be like, "Yeah, I wish I could be that jacked! Grr! Muscles! Power! Yarrgh!"

So criticizing the standards for *both* sexes is totally fair game: either way, it's a yucky byproduct of the patriarchy. (Check out the Hawkeye Initiative, a website where artists around the Internet redraw dude superheroes posing in identical positions to heroines like Psylocke and Catwoman—it's hilarious. Sad, but hilarious.)

# Your New Faves: Kick-Ass Female Characters You Need to Know

There are so many things out there to read and watch and play, and yet so few that can be counted on for decent lady protagonists. Everyone knows Lt. Uhura, and Lara Croft, and Ellen Ripley, and Buffy the effing Vampire Slayer, but what about when you're ready to venture out of reruns and rewatches and into something totally new? How do you start playing video games when this is your first-ever console and every game looks like it's basically a stubbly-sad-white-dude simulator? Which comics can you grab that don't have giant camel-toe splashed across every page? Are there actually genre TV shows with queer or women-of-color characters that don't totally suck? Please? Please.

Avoid the misogynist minefield of modern media, and don't get stuck watching, reading, or playing something dead boring. Here are the best under-the-radar but rad-as-hell female protagonists in movies, TV shows, comics, anime, and video games.

## Comics

### Heroine: Kate Kane

SERIES: *Batwoman*

START HERE→ *Batwoman: Elegy* trade, written by Greg Rucka; continue through New 52 *Batwoman* for 24 issues

If you're looking for a female superhero who isn't all gratuitous physically-impossible-if-you-have-a-spine boob-and-butt shots, then meet army brat Kate Kane: a lovely Jewish girl who is forced to leave the military after she refuses to hide that she's gay. Kate takes up the mantle of Batwoman, giving Bruce Wayne a run for his money (it's funny because they're rich!) with her suave socialite lifestyle and mysterious bat-suited crime fighting. A queer lady, gorgeous ginger, and owner of a Batwoman costume with combat boots instead of insultingly useless high heels? Hell yes. Bonus: writer Greg Rucka has been known to go on vitriolic rants against Fake Geek Girl culture, because he is incredible. Double bonus: the multiple GLAAD-award-winning creative team of J. H. Williams III and W. H. Blackman *walked off the comic* after twenty-four issues when DC refused to let Kate marry her fiancée. Solidarity!

## Heroine: Sonja

SERIES: *Red Sonja*

START HERE→ *Red Sonja* Vol. 1, "Queen of Plagues," by Gail Simone (Image Comics), *Legends of Red Sonja* (Image Comics, 5 issues)

If you like your ladies bad-ass, boozy, and frequently bangin', then you need to up your Red Sonja game, stat. Way before Buffy or Black Cat started beating up baddies, Red Sonja was barbarian-ing it up on the pages of *Conan*. Current writer Gail Simone (one of the best comics writers of our time, just FYI) describes Sonja as "mayhem, blood, sex, and red hair," and "lusty, a bit of a drunkard [who] does what she wants, says what she wants, and if you give her any shit, it's entirely possible she'll slay you and your best friend and your best friend's cat." Yeah. *Yeah.* Start reading about our fave Hyrkanian She-Devil with Simone's series—you can jump right in to all the action from there, no background knowledge required—then check out the five-issue *Legends of Red Sonja*, a series of stand-alone tales written exclusively by the best female writers in the biz (including Tamora Pierce, Kelly Sue DeConnick,

Mercedes Lackey, and Marjorie Liu, just to name a few). And don't worry about that metal bikini. Sonja totally owns it and makes you wish you had one, too.

## Heroines: Carol and Kamala

SERIES: *Captain Marvel* and *Ms. Marvel*

START HERE→ Captian Marvel Vol. 1: "Higher, Further, Faster, More," by Kelly Sue DeConnick; *Ms. Marvel* Vol. 1 "No Normal," by G. Willow Wilson

Carol Danvers started out as a pilot in the Air Force who, after gaining powers like flight and energy beam shooting in an alien explosion, joined the Avengers as Ms. Marvel. Recently, Carol has taken up the Captain Marvel moniker in a new run penned by sass-master Kelly Sue DeConnick, which sees her flying off into space with her cat, Chewie (Carol's a big *Star Wars* fan, obv) and keeping an eye over those pesky Guardians of the Galaxy. Also of interest: Captain Marvel used to be a dude character, and Carol now wears his exact outfit (no heels or boob-windows added). Blonde, beautiful, and bad-ass, Carol can do no wrong in my eyes.

That, of course, has left the Ms. Marvel name free—but we couldn't have *that* for long. Enter Kamala Khan, a fifteen-year-old Muslim Pakistani American in Jersey City, who sneaks out to a party where she accidentally runs into some creepy fog and suddenly finds herself with the power to shape-shift. Kamala is adorable and super nerdy, and she idolizes the Avengers, so she's basically you. It's written by G. Willow Wilson (a Muslim woman) and illustrated by the incredible Adrian Alphona. You've got to follow Kamala's journey of self-discovery and also awkwardness and some detentions and strict parents and superpowers. Best.

## Heroines: Hannah, Violet, Dee, and Betty

SERIES: *Rat Queens*

START HERE→ *Rat Queens* Vol. 1, "Sass and Sorcery," by Kurtis J. Wiebe (Image Comics)

Written by Kurtis Wiebe (who describes it as *Lord of the Rings* meets *Bridesmaids*), published by Image Comics, and nominated for an Eisner Award for best new series of 2014, the Rat Queens are a party of four foul-mouthed, tough-as-nails fantasy adventurer ladies, and they could kick your butt. First, we've got group leader Hannah, a rockabilly Elven mage with amazing tattoo half sleeves and a talent for necromancy. Then there's Violet, the dwarven ginger warrior who shaves her beard because she wants to and not because it's fashionable. Dee is a human cleric of color who's escaped from a Cthulhu-worshipping cult, and Betty is the blonde hippie/Halfling/thief/bartender who really, really loves getting high. The four girls find themselves caught up in some classic medieval fantasy adventures, but their responses are anything but typical. They're basically you and your besties, if you found yourselves in *Skyrim*.

# Television

## Heroine: Helen Magnus

SERIES: *Sanctuary*

START HERE→ Episode 1, "Sanctuary for All"

I literally can't with how deep my love goes for Helen Magnus. Born in 1850, Helen is a lady scientist in Victorian London who works with some folks you may have heard of: Tesla, Watson, even Jack the Ripper. When she and her science bros inject themselves with vampire blood, they each receive a unique power—Helen's is immortality. Fast-forward to present day and Helen has started a worldwide network of safe houses for "abnormals" called Sanctuaries; anyone or anything different or out of the usual can find a home in the Sanctuary network, away from persecution or problems. Helen is super smart, crazy kick-ass, and wickedly philanthropic, and her hair is to die for. Flawless. *Sanctuary* was one of the first webseries ever; it was the first webseries to be successfully ported to television; and it was shot almost entirely on green screen. Amanda Tapping executive produced the show, and she has gone on to become a pioneering woman in the industry as a prolific director, producer, actress, and also my hero.

## Heroines: Xena and Gabrielle

SERIES: *Xena: Warrior Princess*

START HERE→ Episode 1, "Sins of the Past"

It doesn't get much more kick-ass chick than Xena the (mofrickin') Warrior Princess, and if you haven't yet seen this classic series, allow me to persuade you to do so right-damn-now. Filmed in gorgeous pre-Middle-Earth New Zealand, the show follows Lucy Lawless as Xena, a brilliant warrior in mythological ancient Greece (the gods turn up a lot) on a quest for redemption during which she beats up as many dudes as possible with her deadly Moon Tiara Boomerang/chakram. Her trusty sidekick is a naive farm girl named Gabrielle, who, over the course of the show, develops into her own strong warrior woman. (If Xena is Chaotic Neutral, Gabby is definitely Lawful Good.)

A spin-off of the Kevin Sorbo vehicle *Hercules: The Legendary Journey* (which, if you like bodacious shirtless dudes, you might want to check out as well), *Xena* aired from 1995 to 2001, with the janky VFX to prove it. But honestly that's part of the charm; the show never took itself seriously. There are enough ridiculous sound effects, inside jokes, and audience nods to keep you perpetually entertained (thanks, executive producer Sam Raimi). Oh, and Xena and Gabrielle were, like, totally in love with each other. Which was a really big deal for a show in the mid-'90s.

## Heroine: Captain Janeway

SERIES: *Star Trek: Voyager*

START HERE→ Episode 1, "Caretaker"

There's a lot of *Star Trek* out there, but there's only one iteration of the classic franchise that features a female Starfleet captain, and that's *Star Trek: Voyager*. As commander of the USS *Voyager* in 2371, Kathryn Janeway accidentally ends up stranding herself and her crew in the Delta Quadrant (really, really, *really* far away—the only way back to Earth would take them seventy years). *Voyager* follows Janeway (a single gal, for the record) as she attempts to be the best officer and captain she can be while in the terrifying unexplored reaches of space.

Janeway loses fewer crewmembers than Kirk, she's the first captain since Kirk to become an admiral, and no one questions her competence as a Starfleet captain because of her gender. Janeway is also the best because she believes in independence and autonomy at all times—she helps Seven of Nine, a former Borg, regain her humanity, and she is a huge advocate of getting the Doctor, a hologram, recognized as a sentient being. The first two seasons of *Voyager* are pretty meh, but stick it out until Janeway takes her hair out of that questionable updo. It's totally worth it. (Also, I'mma let you finish, but *Voyager* has one of the best theme songs of all time.)

## Heroine: Zoë

SERIES: *Firefly*

START HERE→ Episode 1, "Serenity" (not to be confused with the postseries feature film, *Serenity*)

Okay, so you probably know *of* Zoë. But I'm here to say that you should rewatch *Firefly* and see just how integral Zoë Alleyne Washburne is to its awesomeness. Zoë—one of the crewmembers aboard the spaceship *Serenity* traveling the 'verse doing odd jobs (some legal, mostly not)—is a former soldier and a brilliant markswoman who rules her (interracial!) marriage with sarcasm and a soft-but-still-iron like fist. Her personal journey through the show, film, and subsequent run of plot-continuing comics is tragic, beautiful, and inspiring. (There's also the small fact that only 9 percent of sci-fi shows feature black women as lead characters.) Plus, the actress who plays her—Gina Torres—has been in every genre show from *Cleopatra 2525* to *Xena* to *Buffy*. She's a cultural icon. She could entrance you with her gorgeous face and then kill you with her biceps. Worship her, is essentially what I'm saying here.

# Movies

## Heroine: Chihiro/Sen

MOVIE: *Spirited Away*

From one of the most acclaimed films of Hayao Miyazaki and Studio Ghibli (and probs one of the best animated films of all time, to be perfectly honest), Chihiro Ogino (or, as she is later renamed, Sen) is the ten-year-old protagonist of *Spirited Away*. After discovering that her parents have been turned into pigs and are being transported to a spirit world, Sen has to figure out a way to free both herself and her folks and return to her normal life. Kind of a big deal for a ten-year-old, you know what I mean? Sen's journey over the course of *Spirited Away* is one of true personal growth. She starts out as a regular girl—childish, easily scared, innocent—and ends up reliable, courageous, and secure in the knowledge of the kind of person she really is. Plus, the movie has all the wonderful, quiet, and magical touches that make it a true Miyazaki film. Sen's bravery and responsibility are impressive, and ten-year-olds of all ages can learn a little from her.

## Heroine: Mallory

MOVIE: *Haywire*

Not a lot of people saw *Haywire*, but they *totally should have* because it features one of the most kick-ass female leads in the history of movies. Former MMA fighter (seriously, like, ranked-third-best-in-the-world MMA fighter) Gina Carano plays Mallory Kane, a black ops spy who does some spy-y things and … listen, the plot doesn't really matter here. It's basically *Die Hard* or any other big-budget action flick, but it stars Gina (who does *all* her own stunts) instead of some beefy dude. But if you happen to appreciate beefy dudes, Gina *does* get to star opposite Michael Fassbender, Ewan McGregor, Channing Tatum, and Antonio Banderas. Just sayin'.

## Heroine: Mace

MOVIE: *Strange Days*

Let's talk real quick about director Kathryn Bigelow. This woman is stone-cold amazing: in 2010, she became the first-ever woman to win the Academy Award, DGA, BAFTA, and Critics' Choice Award for best directing for her film *The Hurt Locker*. But years before she got all Oscar-y (and a few years after dumping James Cameron, boom), Bigelow won a Saturn Award for directing her 1995 sci-fi flick *Strange Days*. (She was the first woman to ever win that, too.) *Strange Days* depicts an alternate history in which the biggest craze in 1999 (the future!) is something called "squid," a device that allows you to transmit your thoughts, feelings, and memories into other people's brains. But the hands-down best part of the flick is Angela Bassett as combat specialist Mace, a gun-toting bad-ass who has no problem taking down rooms full of thugs. Bigelow cast Bassett in the role because, prior to *Strange Days*, Bassett had been typecast as a victim (as Tina Turner or Betty Shabazz, for example); with this turn, Bassett was allowed to break out of that stereotype—and break some faces in the process. Aww yiss.

## Heroine: Moon

### MOVIE: *Hero*

This Chinese martial arts (or *wuxia*) film from 2002 is all about assassinations and revenge in ancient China. Technically it stars Jet Li, but that's not what this flick really has going for it. The best part of *Hero* is Zhang Ziyi as Moon. Apprentice to a highly skilled assassin named Broken Sword, Moon is an amazing martial artist in her own right, and her jam is fighting with *twin swords*. (If you think I'm basically talking about Zhang Ziyi flying around slicing people up with double blades while looking hella graceful, then you are *1000 percent correct*, friend.) And—no spoilers—but Moon's final battle is one of the most beautifully shot revenge sequences I've ever seen. Featuring stunning color palettes and gorgeous fan-art-worthy costumes, *Hero* was the most expensive and highest grossing movie in Chinese history when it came out, won tons of critical acclaim upon its release in North America, *and* was nominated for an Oscar, so you have no excuse not to have seen it ten times already.

# Games

## Heroine: April

*The Longest Journey* and *Dreamfall: The Longest Journey*

You can download the original game at www.longest-journey.com, or you can grab both games on Steam.

Maybe the most memorable female character in all of adventure gaming, April Ryan is the protagonist of 1999's *The Longest Journey* and its 2006 follow-up, *Dreamfall*. Rocking jeans and a tee or a gorgeous *Matrix*-esque duster jacket that would make Trinity jealous, April is not only the daughter of a *dragon* but also a Shifter—someone who can move between the normal boring world of Stark and the magical land of Arcadia. Where there are *dragons*. To whom she was *born*, you guys. April's got all the usual adventure business—prophecies about her, fighting the forces of chaos, Catholic guilt—but she's also a no-nonsense lady who forms a band of rebels and prefers to be called Raven or Scorpion, thank you very much. (Also, I think *I* would like to be called Scorpion from here on out.)

## Heroine: Samus

The Metroid series

The most recent *Metroid* is *Other M*, but many people prefer *Metroid Prime 3: Corruption* (both for the Wii).

It's true: the person inside that giant, bulky power armor in those *Metroid* games for Nintendo, aka Samus Aran, the bounty hunter, ex–Galactic Federation soldier, six-foot-three, two-hundred-pound, arm-cannon-toting, space-pirate-hunting Metroid killer is a *lady*. A super fantastic, needs no boob-shaped armor, doesn't even care if you know her gender lady. And I love her. Out to avenge the deaths of her parents at the hands of the evil space pirate Ridley, Samus gained her powers and her suit from the Chozo, the birdlike aliens who adopted her as an orphaned child. Just as powerful in her Zero Suit (which is skintight and shows off her blonde ponytail, but, whatever), Samus is inarguably the most powerful female character in Nintendo's entire roster—which means you should totally use her to kick your friends' asses in *Super Smash Bros.*

## Heroine: Faith

GAME: *Mirror's Edge*

START HERE→ There's only one *Mirror's Edge* game so far (available for PS3, Xbox 360, and PC), but a sequel is in development.

Faith Connors grew up in a totalitarian regime called the City, where she lived a tough life on the streets as a teenager learning to fend for herself. After becoming a Runner—part of an illegal underground courier group—Faith finds herself constantly pursued by the forces of totally evil government dudes. Essentially, Faith is a super-rare mixed-race part-Asian playable character who is basically a master of parkour and free running. She also has sweet martial arts skills, and she knows her way around a gun and some other weapons, too. And in case she wasn't already tough enough for you, Faith rocks a full sleeve and a tattoo under her right eye. So don't mess with her. She'll run you right off a roof.

## Heroine: Liara

GAME: The Mass Effect trilogy

START HERE→ Everyone knows *Mass Effect 2* is the best of the trilogy, but definitely start with the first game (available for PS3, Xbox

360, and PC). You won't be able to get invested in the characters and the story in the same way if you skip the first game.

Is your gaming experience missing some thousand-year-old blue gender-fluid pansexual aliens? Then have I got the game for you! Check out the Mass Effect trilogy. Created by Bioware, the same people who make such excellent fantasy titles as *Baldur's Gate* and *Dragon Age*, *Mass Effect* is a space RPG, in which you can play as a fully customizable male or female character (and your gender choice doesn't affect the story at all!). You also have multiple in-game romance options, one of whom is, of course, the darling Liara T'Soni. An asari alien, Liara is "only" 106 years old (young by asari standards) who starts the game as a brilliant scientist and archaeologist. Liara doesn't differentiate between species or genders when it comes to choosing partners; in fact, she is able to act as the female or the male in procreation. Because all asari are technically biologically female, the society's thousand-year-old matriarchs are revered as wise and mythical creatures (mostly). Also, asari have sweet powers of seduction, and Liara is a master when it comes to using biotics (think mage powers), so there's really absolutely no reason not to like her or her species.

## Heroine: Aveline

GAME: *Assassin's Creed III: Liberation*

START HERE→ Despite the name, you don't need to buy *Assassin's Creed III* to play *Liberation*—the game stands on its own. You can link the games for added bonuses, but you definitely don't have to. *Liberation* is available for PS Vita, PS3, Xbox 360, and PC.

Let's all just bow down to Ubisoft for making the incredible playable female assassin of color that is Aveline de Grandpré. Picture this: it's 1765 New Orleans, and Aveline is the product of a *plaçage* marriage, a temporary union between a French merchant and a freed African slave. In addition to being a secret member of the Assassin Brotherhood (in which she kills all sorts of bad dudes), Aveline is also a super-wicked businesswoman and a respected upper-class biracial lady. She's got no inherent weakness as a woman—the blades hidden up her sleeves help her easily take down rooms full of dangerous men. Oh, and those sleeves? Attached to an outfit without cleavage, boob-cup armor, or high heels. The best. Aveline can also take on a Lady persona, in which she wears a sweet corset and rocks all kinds of bribes, and *did I mention she has a parasol gun*? The game isn't perfect, but Aveline sure as hell is, and that's a good enough reason as any to give it a play.

# Books

## Heroine: Daine

SERIES: *The Immortals* quartet by Tamora Pierce

START HERE→ Book 1, *Wild Mage*

Tamora Pierce was writing high-fantasy books about magical worlds a whole decade before GRRM even dreamed up Westeros, except her stories are better because all of them feature a killer female protagonist. Pierce's second fantasy quartet set in the land of Tortall—and my personal favorite—follows Daine Sarrasri, a girl of color who discovers she has the rare gift of wild magic, which bestows upon her the ability to communicate with animals. Over the course of the series, Daine learns to take control of her powers, becomes the heroine of an entire war, stands up to gods, kings, and knights, doesn't let her lower-class origins stop her from demanding what is right, and protects both humans and animals alike. And she even finds love with an older gentleman whom Pierce based on Jeff Goldblum (I don't know if that will sway many of you, but it certainly works on me!). Daine fans can go back and read Pierce's first Tortall quartet, *The Song of the Lioness*, whose heroine disguises herself as a man to become a knight, and then follow with the *Protector of the Small* quartet, featuring a girl who tries to be the first openly female knight in a century to gain her shield (sensing a theme?). Pierce's other two Tortall series are about girls who are master spies and slum cops, so basically you should probably read all of her books right now. Go. I'll wait.

## Heroine: Gemma Doyle

**SERIES:** The Gemma Doyle Trilogy by Libba Bray

**START HERE→** *A Great and Terrible Beauty*

Libba Bray blew my mind with this evocative and mysterious trilogy that mixes the mystical with the historical in all the right ways. In 1895, Gemma Doyle is a sixteen-year-old British girl living in India when her mother dies under some mysterious-slash-culty-slash-magical circumstances. Shipped back to boarding school in Victorian London, Gemma finds herself confronted with dark magic, enchanted realms, mystical visions, boarding-school girl drama, lady kissing, tempting boys belonging to strange orders, and more. Gemma develops her own powers and her own agency, and there's no doubt she's the heroine of this story. (Once you're done with the Gemma Doyle trilogy, you should also pick up Libba Bray's *Beauty Queens* for a solid dystopian romp that criticizes the crazy standards to which ladies are held.)

## Heroines: Kaede and Taisin

BOOK: *Huntress* by Malinda Lo

There isn't a whole lot of LGBT-friendly YA fantasy lit out there, but Malinda Lo has granted us all our greatest wish with *Huntress*. Taisin is a sage, magically blessed and gifted with prophetic dreams, while Kaede is all about logic and living in the moment. The two girls are sent together on a dangerous journey across their nation to make contact with the mythical Fairy Queen, and on the way they happen to get to know each other. Like, a lot. (They fall in love! It's adorable.) Not only does it have some sweet lady lovin', *Huntress* is also full of references to Chinese culture and mythology, and Taisin's powers are based on the *I Ching*. Also, same-sex attraction is treated like *any* relationship, which is refreshing and important. No one is scandalized by or prohibiting of their love. It's just love! Hooray!

## Heroine: Cimorene

SERIES: *The Enchanted Forest Chronicles* by Patricia C. Wrede

START HERE→ *Dealing with Dragons*

Cimorene, princess of my heart! The youngest daughter of the king of Linderwall, Cimorene is the determined and fearsomely smart girl the Paper Bag Princess would've grown up to be. ("When people were being polite, they said she was strong-minded. When they were angry or annoyed with her, they said she was as stubborn as a pig.") Unwilling to marry a handsome-but-boring prince (and who wouldn't be?), Cimorene braids her hair, packs up her handkerchiefs and her best crown, and heads out to volunteer as the captive of the dragon Kazul; she organizes the dragon's library, keeps tabs on the treasure hoard, and makes a bang-up cherries jubilee. She doesn't hate on girly girls (her BFF Alianora is a much more traditional princess), she melts wizards when they get in her way, and she even thwarts a plan to usurp the throne of King of the Dragons—a title that ends up going to her (female) dragon buddy Kazul. Progressive! The rest of the series follows with more great adventures, charming romance, and something called the Frying Pan of Doom. Probably the only bad thing about Cimorene is when she (spoiler alert) names her son Daystar. But we can't all be perfect.

# Anime

## Heroine: Hawkeye

SERIES: *Fullmetal Alchemist* and *Fullmetal Alchemist: Brotherhood*

START HERE→ Check out "Those Who Challenge the Sun," the first episode of 2003's *Fullmetal Alchemist;* or "Fullmetal Alchemist," the first episode of the 2009 reboot, *Fullmetal Alchemist: Brotherhood.* I watched *Brotherhood* first, but that's just me.

A military officer, kick-ass bodyguard, and 1000 percent done with your shit, Lieutenant Riza Hawkeye is one of several excellent female characters in *Fullmetal Alchemist* and its 2009 remake, *Fullmental Alchemist Brotherhood.* In a world where everyone uses alchemy (essentially magic) to fight their battles, Hawkeye has no time for your games and just gets the job done with *every gun.* She's on equal footing with the men she works with, never gets creepily sexualized, and has both an epic back tattoo and a bunch of burn scars that only add to her killer vibe. And let's not forget that *Fullmetal Alchemist* also features non-gender-binary characters, a visibly disabled protagonist, a visibly disabled impoverished woman of color with a rocket launcher in her prosthetic limb, a miniature pet panda (!), persons of color with mental health issues, and a narrative criticizing racism, imperialism, and white-male-dominated power structures. Oh, and it was written by a lady. If you're not impressed by all of that, you're wrong.

## Heroine: Mikasa

SERIES: *Attack on Titan* (sometimes known by the Japanese title *Shingeki no Kyojin*, or *SNK*)

START HERE→ Episode 1 "To You, in 2000 Years—The Fall of Shiganshina, Part 1." It's got a sub and a dub, so it's up to you, though all the crazy yelling in this show does sound particularly awesome in Japanese.

A mixed-race girl who happens to be the last person of Asian descent inside the Wall (where everyone she knows lives, because, you know, outside the Wall are huge terrifying monsters called Titans, *guys, keep up*), Mikasa joined the Survey Corps as a soldier after escaping from traffickers who wanted to sell her to the highest bidder. The top soldier in her graduating class, Mikasa is no-nonsense and bad-ass—she can literally fight off gigantic monsters and human slavers with equal success—but she also loves hard and has a lot of feels. She's got a strong moral compass and just wants to live in peace, but she knows she has to stand up for what she believes in, and that makes her p. rad in my book. (And she's super cute. I want to be her.) Bonus: the character Zoë Hange, a wicked-brilliant scientist who, despite having a traditionally female first name, is actually never gendered. *Attack on Titan* creator Hajime Isayama has specifically requested that the character remain non-binary; in the English dub, Hange is referred to in equal amounts as both "he" and "she." Oh, and Hange rocks some sweet specs, too.

## Heroine: Motoko

SERIES: *Ghost in the Shell*

START HERE→ *Ghost in the Shell: Stand Alone Complex*, then its second season *S.A.C. 2nd GIG*, then the film *Solid State Society*

Just when you thought women in anime couldn't get any radder, *think again*, because let's talk about Major Motoko Kusanagi from *Ghost in the Shell*. Living in a post-cyberpunk alternate-twenty-first-century Japan, Motoko is the head of the counter-cyberterrorist organization Public Security Section 9. Not satisfied with taking down evil hackers on the reg, Motoko is also a cyborg (damn, girl, slow down), living in a fully cybernetic body since a childhood accident. Her artificial body is also compatible with other cyborgs of both male and female gender, totally making her an awesome bisexual lady protagonist. Because who doesn't want more bi robot ladies in their TV shows? Yes, her outfit includes a really uncomfortable-looking thong, but the fact that she can fight cybercrime while ignoring the urge to yank that perpetual wedgie out of her butt is proof enough that Motoko is a true heroine.

## Heroine: Lina

SERIES: *Slayers*

START HERE→ *Slayers* episode 1, "ANGRY? Lina's Furious Dragon Slave!"

If you're more into magic than cybercrime, don't even worry, lady-bros, because have I got the girl for you. Teenage sorceress Lina Inverse is the lead in *Slayers*, one of the most popular anime of the '90s, and the most powerful and famous sorceress in the world (and at only fifteen years old that's, like, a pretty big deal). Her extreme use of black magic—like that one time she turned an entire ocean into a literal *sea of death*—means that Lina has to eat all the time (how can I get this power, stat?). She's really afraid of only her older sister and slugs—her older sister being Luna, an equally awesome Knight of Ceifeed who wields so much holy power that she once defeated a *plasma dragon* with a *kitchen knife*. (Can that be the next battle in *The Elder Scrolls Online*, please? Thanks so, so much in advance.) Finally, Lina's also a savvy businesswoman, in case you needed more reason to like her.

# Everyone's a Critic and So Can You

All that is gold does not glitter, not all who wander are lost, and no piece of media can stay perfect (except Joss Whedon's timeless cinematic masterpiece *Serenity*). Nope, not even the things you love (unless that thing is *Serenity*). Maybe your favorite series changed show runners and got way worse, or the best New 52 title got a new artist, or the movie adaptation left out all the important bits of the book. Or maybe something even worse happened, like an otherwise excellent show making a serious misstep about the representation of minorities, or one creator attacking another with terrible sexist rants. When crumminess happens to your fandom, you'll want to complain about it online. And, you *should*.

It's important to critically evaluate everything you read, watch, or play—even if it's created by other gals. (Society's awkward institutionalized misogyny thing means women are completely capable of creating lady characters that might uphold sexist standards, unforch.) That's not to say you can't also be totally into things, even when they're not perfect. (I'm not telling you to boycott every single game with a plaid-shirted angsty white male protagonist, or to stop reading your guilty-pleasure YA romance novels!) But being critical of media you enjoy and expressing your criticism in positive and helpful ways is the perfect method to get a larger audience to understand the problems at hand.

The fancy academic term for enjoying media despite its occasional problems is "critical distance," which is exactly what it sounds like—that moment when you step back, consider, and write a great blog post about some of the things that particular text, show, or comic could have done better. Critical distance allows you to start a dialogue about things you actually like, too, which is way better than making a giant post about something you hate.

Not sure if what you're watching or reading holds up to fangirl feminist standards? Here are some things to look out for when being a critical consumer of comics and other media.

## Does it pass the Bechdel Test?

Created by artist Alison Bechdel, the test is simple: if the film has (1) two named female characters, (2) who talk to each other, (3) about something other than a man, it passes. Sounds pretty easy, but you would be shocked at just how many pieces of media fail the test. But the Bechdel Test isn't foolproof! Lots of people think *Pacific Rim* is a wonderfully feminist, female-empowering film, but it doesn't pass the Bechdel test. Moreover, this is not a litmus test; although it can be handy to apply to individual films, it is more useful in aggregate (i.e., LOOK AT HOW FEW FILMS PASS THIS TEST! WE MUST CHANGE THINGS! FEMINIST HULK SMASH!).

## Does a female character get "fridged"?

"Fridging" is a term coined by comics writer Gail Simone after she read an issue of *Green Lantern* in which the titular hero comes home to find that his girlfriend has been killed and stuffed in the fridge. When a woman is "fridged," it means that she has been killed or harmed for the plot or character advancement of a dude. Did you guys see *Thor: The Dark World*? Remember how a woman who's important to Thor and Loki gets murdered, and that forces the brothers to work together and grow and stuff? That's fridging. Uncool.

## How healthy is that relationship, anyway?

There's a lot of media out there (like *Twilight* and *50 Shades of Grey*) that glorifies abusive, controlling, or even violent behavior as a romantic relationship. When we read these books and think, "Wow, that's so sweet that he shows up at her house, uninvited, at night, while she's unconscious, to watch her sleep!" we subconsciously accept that behavior as okay. If a guy ever calls a woman rude names or insults, acts in a way that scares her, stops her from seeing her friends or family, insists on making all the decisions, destroys her things or threatens her pets, threatens to kill himself if she leaves him, damages property when angry, abandons her in a dangerous or unfamiliar place, purposefully drives recklessly, views women as objects, frequently accuses her of cheating, or is often extremely jealous of her male friends, all that counts as domestic abuse—even if he never physically harms her. Not romantic. Not at all.

## Does the female character find herself kidnapped or in need of saving by the Heroic Lead Male?

Then she's been "damseled" (as in, damsel in distress). This plot line perpetuates the stereotype that women are weak and need a dude to rescue them, and we all know that's just not true.

## Are the sexy costumes truly empowering, or are they just exploitative?

There's nothing worse than a piece of misogynist media lurking in feminist disguise. But sometimes it's hard to find the line between empowerment and exploitation, and just because a creator or writer *says* something is progressive doesn't always mean that it is. It all comes down to agency—who's making the choices and why. If a lady-fighter character finds out that she can harness her true powers only when she embraces her sexy outfit (complete with boob windows, high-cut leg holes, and heels), that might seem like body positivity, but it's not really a fair choice. Our friend isn't choosing to wear the outfit because it makes her feel rad as hell; she's just resigned herself to being a sex object because the alternative is no power at all. Tricky, but see how easy it would be to stop at "Seems pretty empowering, let's roll with it"? That's why we are using our awesome critical thinking hats (mine has feathers).

## Is the villain's chief evil power a sexy evil power?

Any time an evil lady villain (aliens disguised as sexy ladies in order to entrap men, demon vampire bitches, you know the type) uses her sexuality to prey on the poor men in the film (who have no defense against her sexalicious feminine wiles, of course), it reinforces the idea that female sexuality and sexual freedom are scary and evil and should be restrained at all costs because *who will think of the men????* Not cool! Sometimes we just wanna have sex and not have anyone die from it!

## Is there Just One Girl in a cast of many?

Tokenism—that thing where there's, like, a whole cast full of dudes and then the one lady character in there, just to be like, "Oh, well, yeah, we have a lady, so you can't complain"—is pretty crap. Essayist and critic Katha Pollitt called this phenomenon the "Smurfette Principle" after she noticed the gender disparity in kids' shows, but the same applies to pretty much everything. "The" girl on the show? No good.

## Is there a Manic Pixie Dream Girl?

You know the one: the super-quirky, one-dimensional, impossibly bubbly lady with no story of her own and no real personality. The MPDG exists only to teach the male protagonist a lesson about himself or about life; then the MPDG floats away on a cloud and the guy has totally learned a lesson. But she doesn't get anything out of it—she's a stock character who only exists to further a dude's story (or, in other words, she's a prop).

# So You Want to Critique It...but How?

Making your complaints into something positive and productive is key. And you can use your fandom as a jumping-off point to start a serious discussion about a larger issue. Everybody wins!

## Cool the flames.

Posting hate is useless; you'll just slowly begin to transform into one of the mindless trolls stalking the Internet for prey (and attract trolls of your own). Righteous indignation is okay. ALL CAPS SHOUTY POSTS are not.

## Think of a better way.

Go ahead and write a Tumblr post on why you think an issue is so prevalent in the media, but then also suggest steps that can be taken to fix the problem. If enough people in fandom start making serious inquiries into what's wrong, eventually the mainstream media will pick up on it, and awareness often leads to change. The more conscious and critical you are as a fangirl, the better you'll be able to appreciate the things you love.

## Call out the haters...

Fandoms should be open to everyone, and it's not cute when fans start getting cliquey. If you see anyone being exclusionary, rude, or intentionally misunderstanding of others in online discussions, call them out on it. Be polite, and don't get too harsh too soon—chances are, the fan acting poorly might not even realize that what he or she is doing or saying is hurtful. You could turn things around with a quick message ("I'm sure you didn't mean it this way, but using that word can be offensive") and you might make a new fangirl friend in the process.

Although it's a really good thing to call out faults in the content you care about, be sure to focus your criticisms on that content and *not* the people who make it. When your attacks start getting personal, that's when you start damaging your fandom. Even if you think Steven Moffat has driven *Doctor Who*'s female characters into the ground, don't badmouth him personally; instead, focus on *Clara*'s lack of character development and personality. (Moffat might be showrunner, but he certainly isn't responsible for writing every single episode starring Jenna Coleman.)

Fandom outcry over a misrepresented character or poorly planned plotline might get back to the creators, but don't beat a path to their door (or Twitter account, or Tumblr) full of vitriol and meanness. Instead, work with other fans to raise awareness as a group. Creators and executives are far more likely to take criticism seriously if it's part of a multifan online movement (as opposed to your lone RANTYCAPS post).

# Strong Female Character: Putting Your Feminism into Action

Oh, hey there, *cool ladybro*. Look at you, being all fangirly and feministy. I love it. Now that you know what it means to be a great geek feminist and a fantastic critical thinker about issues of sexism, why don't we take a look at some of the things you can do to put your feminism into action?

## Buy and support female-created media!

Women are still astonishingly underrepresented as directors, writers, and artists in all forms of media, so when we get a good one, we need to support her. The more we drive our hard-earned dollars toward lady-made media, the more ladies will (hopefully) start getting hired.

## Volunteer for a female-centric nonprofit!

There are so many fantastic organizations that help women in geekdom, like Dress for Success and Girls Who Code. If you have some free time, why not donate a few hours to improving the lives of other ladies in the nerd world? Even something like being a Big Sister to a girl can make a *huge* difference.

## Be a role model!

We start learning what it means to be a "girl" from the second we're born, and tons of well-intentioned things condition the way we think about ourselves: gendering toys pink and blue, complimenting girls on their looks instead of their intelligence, treating girls like dolls instead of people. Don't do it. Buy girls LEGOs from the "boy" aisle, tell girls they're "smart" instead of "sweet," ask them what they like to read. Take your little niece out to the natural history museum for dinosaur time and then paint her toenails red while watching *Star Trek*. Same goes for boys: teach them it's wrong to hit anyone, not just girls, and let them play with Barbies if they want. The next generation thanks you.

## Use preferred gender pronouns!

Gender pronouns are words that refer to the person you're talking to (like "she," "him," "hers," or "his") but not everyone is cool with the pronouns you might assume they'd like. If you're unsure, it's okay to ask; once you know what the person likes, always use that set of pronouns (and never as "it"! That's for things, not people). There are also gender-neutral pronouns that some people prefer, like "they/them" or "ze/hir."

## Be intersectional!

This just means listening to and respecting people of all backgrounds. After all, feminism isn't just for the type of person you are. It's for everyone, and you can't really look at oppression without considering race, gender, sexuality, ethnicity, ability, and class. Make sure your feminism includes people of color, queer folks, those of different classes, the trans community, people who might be differently abled, all of the everyone. We all matter!

## Be proud to be like other girls!

I think all us nerdy gals have, at one point, fallen down the internalized misogyny pit of "Oh, I'm not like *other* girls, *girly girls* are the worst," because we've been taught that being interested in traditionally feminine things like beauty makes us dumb or shallow. See how that's messed up? Remember, other women are not your competition. Putting down or refusing to support other ladies just to boost your own profile is venturing into troll territory. We're all here for one another, and that's the way it should be—like the Sailor Senshi, but without the sparkly transformation sequences (if only!).

## Call out misogyny!
It's just like at the train station: "If you see something, say something." If you witness an act of sexism or find something misogynist in media, speak up about it. If we all make our voices loud enough, eventually people and corporations will start listening.

## Value yourself and the things you create!
You are important. You are strong, and brave, and beautiful, and amazing, and you *matter*. Don't ever let anyone devalue what you do, the things you believe, or who you are. You're awesome and your opinions are valid. Believe that!

> **Now, off into the world with you, newly minted geek feminists! Go forth and build the future!**

Interviews with

**Kate Leth,**

**Laura Kate Dale,**

**Victoria Schwab,**

**and  Cynthia Loyst**

# KATE LETH

◇ ◇ ◇

creator of Kate or Die!, writer
for Bravest Warriors, founder
of the ladies-working-in-comic-
shops collective the Valkyries

@KateLeth

## What does the word "fangirl" mean to you?

It's all about enthusiasm. Geek culture stems from an absolute, unabashed love of the things that speak to you. It's the thing I get the most from, whether it's about comics, movies, video games, food, whatever! I'm a fangirl through and through. I freak out when I get to meet people who inspire me. I go to midnight premieres. I have a drawer of nerdy-reference T-shirts. I love being part of a world that encourages excitement.

## How has being a geek positively influenced your life?

In every possible way. Reading Archie got me into trying more comics. Reading comics got me into making them. That's my career now, my friend group, my lifestyle! I was a sad, bored, underachieving college dropout before I started working in a shop and making comics on the Internet. I'm still a college dropout, but I'm writing comics for a living and traveling all over the world to conventions or to visit friends I met through the nerd world. It's been amazing and I'm incredibly lucky.

## What advice can you give geek girls for their careers or personal lives?

Don't let anyone tell you not to love the things you love. There are gatekeepers and elitists and chauvinists in every industry, but there are way more good people than bad. Find your people. If you're a creator of any kind, that's even more important. Find your crew of weirdos. Make friends and allegiances. Cosplay as the inner senshi. Rejoice.

# LAURA KATE DALE

◊ ◊ ◊

founding member of Indie Haven.com; developer of the game You Are the Reason; contributor to the *Guardian*, Kotaku UK, MCM Buzz, and more

@LauraKBuzz

### What does the word "fangirl" mean to you?

A fangirl is someone who knows what they love and is not ashamed to show their passion in the hopes of finding people to share that love with. You know that the things you love are not perfect, but you love them anyway.

### How has being a geek positively influenced your life?

From traveling to events and talking to creators of my favorite games to becoming part of active groups on Twitter, being a geek has helped put up big signposts leading me and other likeminded geeks together. I've spoken to people across the world about the things I like, the things I hate, the things I'm not sure about, and everything else I experience. I love knowing that if I hate the new episode of *Doctor Who* I can not only find people to share my pain, but I can also encounter people who did like it and learn where we differed.

### What advice can you give geek girls for their careers or personal lives?

Speak to the geek girls you look up to online and let them know how much you love their work. We were all once where you are today, wanting to love our favorite things without getting hate for invading "boy spaces." We love to hear that our work makes people happy, and we're always excited to help out the next generation of kickass geek girls to be as awesome as possible.

# VICTORIA SCHWAB

◇ ◆ ◇

author of so many awesome
novels including *Vicious* and the
*Archived* series

@veschwab

### What does the word "fangirl" mean to you?

It's a badge of honor. It means being passionate enough about something that not only do you want to enjoy it, and connect with others who enjoy it, but you also feel an intense need to introduce it to others. You are an emissary, a missionary, converting new people to the fandom wherever you can. There are far joys greater than inducting new members to your ranks.

### How has being a geek positively influenced your life?

The best part of being a geek is that you're never alone. Whatever you love, whatever you geek out over, there are others who geek out over it, too. I've found community in unlikely places, and around unlikely things. And the positive reinforcement of realizing I'm not alone in my passion has helped me to *be* passionate, to be myself. When I was younger, I shied away from showing too much enthusiasm about the things I loved because I was afraid; now I'm louder than ever about the things I love. And I hope I've inspired younger girls to be loud, too.

### What advice can you give geek girls for their careers or personal lives?

Own your geekness. Embrace it. Share it. You are a planet; you have mass and gravity and orbit. Don't shut people out, but don't change who you are just to draw them in. The ones who get you will drift into your atmosphere. The ones who don't get you are space clutter; let them drift on and find their own orbit.

# CYNTHIA LOYST

◇ ◆ ◇

geeky sex and relationship expert and host of CTV's *The Social* and formerly of Space's *InnerSpace*

@CynthiaLoyst

### What does the word "fangirl" mean to you?

A "fangirl" is someone who regularly finds herself fantasizing about being in another world. In other words, as a fangirl I often imagine myself hanging out with (or making out with) characters from imaginary lands.

### How has being a geek positively influenced your life?

First, being into geeky content has always massaged my imagination and creative spirit like nothing else. I've become a warrior in the magical kingdom of Hyrule; I've imagined how I would survive in a postapocalyptic, zombie-ridden world; and I've tried to pin down which location and time (and Doctor) I would choose if I ever find myself in a TARDIS.

Second, being a geek has allowed me to tap into my masculine side. When I was growing up, females were portrayed as weak and/or in need of being saved. So whenever I was playing *Star Wars* or *Battle of the Planet* or *Superfriends*, I would almost always choose a male role. I feel like that helped me grow into a woman who is in touch with her feminine and her masculine sides. (Having said that, I've been happy to witness more fully rounded female characters in the geek world in recent years.)

Last, I think it was definitely a draw for my geeky significant other. He was so delighted that he found a girl who liked video games!

### What advice can you give geek girls for their careers or personal lives?

It's okay to be critical of things in geek culture. Continue to do what you do, like what you like, and ignore anyone who tries to shame you for not seeing things the way they do.

# Resources

## The Best Geek Girl–Friendly Sites You'll Want to Stay on Until 4 a.m.

Sure, anyone can hang out on general nerdy sites like io9 and Think-Geek, but what about those Internet spaces that cater specifically to you, the fangirl? Here's a list of my favorite online resources for geek gals. Just don't blame me when your wallet goes empty or you find yourself scrolling well past bedtime.

## NEWS, NEW IDEAS, AND NEW FRIENDS

### The Mary Sue
www.themarysue.com
If you're a geek girl and you're on the Internet, you should be hitting up the Mary Sue. TMS promotes, watchdogs, extols, and celebrates women's representation in nerdery, tech, and science; it's an inclusive community (the comments sections on each article are a haven of intelligent discussion). Full disclosure: I am an editor for TMS, but only because I love it SO MUCH.

### The Nerdy Girlie
www.thenerdygirlie.com
Fabulous fellow fangirl Megan Gotch runs this blog, which is super amazing for everyday cosplay tips, and has a fantastic guide to getting the most out of San Diego Comic Con.

### Blonde Nerd

www.blondenerd.com

Britt Bombacher is a video game blogger and vlogger who totally wants to chat with you about gaming. Her site is great for lady-friendly articles and videos about games and gaming culture.

### On Wednesdays We Wear Pink

www.wearpinkwednesdays.com

Kristin and Kristin (yep, both of 'em) teamed up to create OWWWP for girls who are both geeky and glam. If you're sci-fi savvy but also into cupcakes and crafting, this is the place for you.

### Black Girl Nerds

www.blackgirlnerds.com

Created by Jamie Broadnax, Black Girl Nerds is a community where nerdy women of color (and everyone else, too) can feel welcomed and included. The site embraces all cultures and allows ladies to express their true selves.

### International Geek Girl Pen Pals

www.geekgirlpenpals.com

Do you love geek culture and snail mail? Then sign up for the IGGPP program, where you're matched up with another girl based on similar interests. I've done this and received a beautiful handmade card from a Floridian fangirl (also, oddly enough, named Sam).

## YOUTUBERS

### ALB

www.youtube.com/albinwonderland

Known for her fab bubblegum pink locks and equally fab feminism, ALB (or Angelina) makes great videos about style and fangirl culture. Her response to the Fake Geek Girl phenomenon is amaze, as are her "Shit Tumblr Girls Say" videos.

## Amy Dallen

www.youtube.com/amydallen

A vlogger on geek girl goddess Felicia Day's YouTube channel Geek & Sundry, Amy talks about comics, like, all the time. She works in a comic book store and can relate just about anything to comics—her show is even called "Amy Dallen Talkin' Comics."

## Vi Hart

www.youtube.com/Vihart

Victoria Hart is a "recreational mathematician" who creates amazing videos that make math accessible, interesting, and (for real) hilarious. Her "Doodling in Math Class" series is worth a watch!

## Lucahjin

www.youtube.com/lucahjin

Otherwise known as Reese, Lucahjin shows playthroughs on her Let's Play channel and streams games live on video site Twitch. She's known for streaming particularly adorbs games, usually made by Nintendo, and is also a pretty great artist. (And she has no filter. You'll like her.)

## TECH TALK

### The Women's Coding Collective

www.thewc.co

The WCC is a Boston-based organization that wants to narrow the gender gap in tech (hooray!). For $50, you can take your pick from a variety of two-week online courses, including CSS, SEO, Java, Wordpress, and more!

## GirlGeeks

www.girlgeeks.org

A great online community for ladies interested in technology and computing, GirlGeeks has info on education and careers, and it even highlights a Girl Geek of the Week!

## Shiny Shiny

www.shinyshiny.tv

Launched in 2004 as the first-ever site aimed at women who love tech, UK site Shiny Shiny brings you news on the latest tech and how it might change your daily life.

## Girl Develop It

www.girldevelopit.com

If you want to learn how to develop software, Girl Develop It wants to help. They've got chapters all across America that run classes and events, and their website has a great resources section filled with tutorials.

## How to Theme

howtotheme.tumblr.com

Ever dream of creating your own spiffy Tumblr theme? The free e-book on this site breaks down everything you need to know, from the basic uses of HTML and CSS elements to more advanced options for infinite scrolling, grid layouts, and group blogs.

# CLOTHES SHOPPING

### Her Universe
www.heruniverse.com
Awesome actress Ashley Eckstein (aka Ahsoka Tano in *Star Wars: The Clone Wars*) started this clothing company for female sci-fi fans. Pick up cute themed dresses, leggings, and more (the *Star Wars* and *Doctor Who* lines especially rock).

### GoldBubble
www.goldbubbleclothing.com
A super-small company (only two people!), GoldBubble has a great range of leggings, dresses, and skirts for every body type. Their Han Solo, Captain America, and *Last Unicorn* collections are killer.

### WeLoveFine
www.welovefine.com
For fans, by fans. WeLoveFine carries an amazing array of geek girl-friendly clothes and accessories that cover everything you love, including *Adventure Time*, *Homestuck*, Marvel, and more.

### Suckers Apparel
www.suckersapparel.myshopify.com
Amazing leggings, dresses, bodysuits, and bathing suits, handmade by one amazing geek girl in Toronto. My faves are her Black Widow, Hawkeye, and Captain Marvel leggings.

### BlackMilk
www.blackmilkclothing.com
Australia-based BlackMilk offers a selection of leggings and dresses you can't find anywhere else, with collections ranging from *Mass Effect* to Batman.

### Activate Apparel

www.activateapparel.com

If you (like myself) need that extra push to get to the gym, Activate's great geeky workout wear might just do it. Join the Sailor Jupiter Lifting Team or rock the "Quidditch is my cardio" tank!

## STYLE ADVICE

### Fashionably Geek

www.fashionablygeek.com

With amazing contributors like Amy Ratcliffe, Nicole Wakelin, and Geek Girl Diva, Fashionably Geek is a wonderful resource for the best in cosplay and nerdy fashion.

### Set to Stunning

www.settostunning.com

Nerdy ladies Lindz and Scruffy run this amazing blog, dedicated to fashionable geek girl styles, fanmade accessories, and their own awesome DIYs.

### White Hot Room

www.whitehotroom.com

Super-fashionable fangirls Bria and Lin share their personal geek-inspired outfits on one of the best everyday cosplay blogs. Their theme weeks (like Hawkeye or Black Widow Week) are especially great.

# BEAUTY PRODUCTS

### CutePolish
www.youtube.com/user/cutepolish
The very best series of YouTube videos for girls looking to get into the nail art game. Super-simple tutorials for even the clumsiest of polishers (we've all been there).

### The Nailasaurus
www.thenailasaurus.com
A UK nail art blog run by a girl named Sammi, who does geek-inspired nail art with easy-to-follow tutorials, like ones for the Avengers.

### Espionage Cosmetics
www.espionagecosmetics.com
A makeup company for nerds by nerds, with colors inspired by *Firefly*, *Game of Thrones*, and more.

### 8BitCosmetics
www.etsy.com/shop/EightBitCosmetics
A makeup line for nerdy ladies, including shades like "Ooh, Shiny," and "Brightest Day." Creator Nicole loves her work and her customers, so you're guaranteed to end up shiny and happy.

### YumeLacquer
www.etsy.com/shop/YumeLacquer
Handmade indie nail polishes inspired by manga, sci-fi, and video games. Shop mistress Amanda takes her inspiration from "female characters in video games. Some strong, some sneaky, some damsels in distress—all have their own quirks and things that make them unique and memorable." Um, perf.

# TUTORIALS

## Commander Holly

www.youtube.com/CommanderHolly

Holly Conrad is cosplay famous: she was featured in Morgan Spurlock's *Comic-Con Episode IV: A Fan's Hope* and now stars on Syfy's *Heroes of Cosplay*. On her YouTube channel, she posts videos called "Cosplay Class," a great how-to on everything from getting started to making gigantic molds.

## CosplayTutorial

www.cosplaytutorial.com

Ever the cosplayer's best friend, CosplayTutorial has everything from wig detangling tips to a Convention Packing Checklist generator.

## Punished Props

www.props.punishedpixels.com

This site has articles, videos, and Q&As on every type of cosplay and prop-making query your nerdy heart could desire. Punished Props is your cosplay *senpai*.

## CosplayResources

www.cosplayresources.tumblr.com

With lots of great tags (including #beginner and #basics), this blog can get you started on your road to cosplay. It crowdsources some great tips for those of you in the know, too. Check out other great cosplay blogs on Tumblr: cosplayguide, helpingcosplay, cosplaying-on-a-budget, and youcancosplay21.

# SUPPLIES AND SUCH

### Arda Wigs
www.arda-wigs.com
With a huge selection of colors and styles at totally reasonable prices, Arda is a great bet for cosplay wigs. The site also features a bunch of handy tutorials for tricky things like clipping on heavy wigs, wig washing, and painting designs on wigs.

### Cosplay.com Marketplace
www.cosplay.com/marketplace
You can buy and sell anything you've ever wanted as a cosplayer on the Marketplace. Lots of pro cosplayers also post ads for commissions, so it's a good place to hunt down a custom-made version of that elusive accessory.

### CosTrader
www.costrader.com
One more excellent marketplace for buying and selling your cosplay goodies. CosTrader has an easy-to-use, image-centric layout, and the prices are usually affordable.

### The Replica Prop Forum
www.trpf.com
If you need to make a prop, chances are someone on RPF has already done it. Check out the boards for tons of tips, or register for an account and ask the experts yourself. The amazing pros on the boards are great at answering any and all of your cosplay Qs.

### Underworks.com
www.underworks.com
Every kind of foundation, compression, or support undergarment

you could imagine, because a good base to your cosplay is important. Underworks also has great items for Rule 63 (aka "gender swap") cosplayers who might wish to play down certain male or female anatomical features.

## PARTY PLANNING TIPS

### The Geeky Hostess
www.thegeekyhostess.com
Tara Theoharis runs this site, where you can find everything to make your space the perfect place for a nerdy party night. She even makes her own line of sprinkles for geeky-sweet baking projects.

### That's Nerdalicious
www.thatsnerdalicious.com
It's like Fashionably Geek, except for things that are delicious! Looking for a Batman cookie recipe or a Mario Kart cake? This is the place.

### Nerdy Nummies
www.youtube.com/RosannaPansino
Rosanna Pansino's YouTube channel is full of nerdy recipes and baking tips to help you create the perfect nerdy desserts. *Animal Crossing* birthday cakes (!), *Divergent* Dauntless cakes (!!), and even Mountain Dew Dorito cupcakes (!!!) await you on her channel.

### The Drunken Moogle
www.thedrunkenmoogle.com
If you're hosting a nerdy night, you're going to want to theme your beverages for the occasion. Enter the Drunken Moogle, where

mixologists have put together easy-to-follow recipes for every-thing from a blue *Tron* drink to a *Borderlands 2* assassin cocktail. They even have nonalcoholic options and drinking games on offer. In fact, I think I'm headed there right now.

# Thank you, thank you, thank you...

To Teddy Wilson, because without your love, support, and sandwich deliveries, I wouldn't have survived the book-writing process. Ot.

To Maria Vicente, the best agent in the 'verse, because you found me, made me into an author, and helped shape this book. And to Maria's cat, Willow, whose butt makes all our Skype calls more enjoyable.

To Blair Thornburgh, editrix extraordinaire, because you not only championed this book, but also took my incoherent feminist ranting and made it into something actually good.

To Andie Reid for your awesome design, and to Kelly Bastow for your beautiful illustrations. This book would be a shadow of itself without your brilliant designs.

To the incredibly inspiring team at the Mary Sue, because I am consistently honored to be working with all of you.

To Karyn Hepburn (*Stargate*), Elena Iosef (*Smallville*), Meghan Campbell (*Game of Thrones*), Soha Kareem (*Garnet*), Emma Fissenden (*Troy Baker*), Danny McMurray (*Nellie McClung*), Rachel Wharton (*Joss Whedon*), Sarah Wild (*anger*), and all of the other fangirls who bring me so much joy every day of my life. Because I love you.

To all of the amazing friends and fangirls I've met on teh internetz; you are all way more talented than I am, and I'm lucky to know you. And to the long-distance friends who messaged me day and night for my sanity—you know who you are, and my thanks is endless.

To the Rosedale Starbucks (and your delicious, constant stream of samples), because I made this book inside of you. Ew.

To Guillermo del Toro, Ramin Djawadi, and Tom Morello, because I wrote this whole damn book to the *Pacific Rim* theme on repeat.

To BioWare, because I wouldn't be a gamer without *Baldur's Gate*, and I wouldn't have been able to finish this book without the Mass Effect trilogy.

And to you, fangirl. You keep doing you. And thanks for reading.